perfect pies

perfect pies

The Best Sweet and Savory Recipes
from America's Pie-Baking Champion

MICHELE STUART

BALLANTINE BOOKS
NEW YORK

ISBN 978-0-345-52488-1
eISBN 978-0-345-52490-4

Printed in China on acid-free paper

www.ballantinebooks.com

4 6 8 9 7 5

Book design by Diane Hobbing

For my beloved grandmother—

I told you I'd make your pies famous some day!

And to my mom, who supported

all of my earliest

pie-making adventures

Contents

Introduction•xi

Kitchen Tools•xvi

Crusts and Toppings•3
. . . .

Traditional Pastry Piecrust•5

Graham Cracker Crust•10

Oreo Cookie Crust•11

Cinnamon Sugar Crumb Topping•12

Macadamia-Coconut Crumb Topping•13

Walnut Crumb Topping•14

Farm Stand Pies•17
. . . .

Country Apple Pie•19

Sugar-Free Apple Pie•21

Apple-Cranberry Crumb Pie•23

Blackberry Pie•25

Blueberry Pie•27

Sugar-Free Blueberry Pie•30

Blueberry-Blackberry Crumb Pie•32

Cherry Pie•34

Sour Cherry Crunch Pie•37

Lemon Meringue Pie•39

Peach Crumb Pie•43

Peach-Blueberry Pie•45

Pear Pie•47

Pear-Raspberry Pie•49

Pear-Apple-Cranberry Crumb Pie•51

Pear-Cranberry Pie with Walnut Crumb•53

Pineapple Crumb Pie•55

Pineapple-Mango Pie with Macadamia-Coconut Crumb•57

Pumpkin Pie•59

Maple Pumpkin Pie with Pecan Streusel•62

Pumpkin Chiffon Pie•66

Raspberry Crumb Pie•69

Rhubarb Pie•71

Strawberry-Rhubarb Crumb Pie•73

Sweet Potato Pie•75

Nut Pies•79
. . . .

Pecan Pie•81

Chocolate-Pecan-Bourbon Pie•83

Caramel-Chocolate-Pecan Pie•86

Chocolate Walnut Pie•88

Maple Walnut Pie•90

Raisin Crunch Pie•92

Maple Oatmeal Raisin Pie•94

Cream Pies•97
. . . .

Boston Cream Pie•99

Chocolate Cream Pie•102

Chocolate–Peanut Butter Dream Pie•104
Chocolate-Raspberry Delight Pie•107
Banana Cream Pie•109
Mom's Banana-Coconut Delight Pie•111
Coconut Custard Pie•114
Coconut Cream Pie•116
Coffee–Heath Bar Crunch Pie•118
Key Lime Pie•120
Lemon Chiffon Pie•122
Strawberry Glacé Pie•124
Twisted Citrus Blackberry Pie•127

Party Pies•131
. . . .

Ultimate Banana Split Pie•133
Candy Apple Crumb Pie•135
Candyland Pie•137
Eggnog Cream Pie•141
Crunchy Ice Cream Pie•143
Michele's Mud Pie•144
S'mores Delight Pie•145
Tiramisù Pie•147

Savory Pies•151
. . . .

Chicken Pot Pie•153
Australian Beef Pie•156
Lobster Pot Pie•158

Quiche Lorraine•161

Broccoli and Cheddar Quiche•163

Ham and Brie Quiche•165

Lobster Quiche•167

Sausage and Provolone Quiche•169

Spinach and Asparagus Quiche•171

Zucchini and Tomato Quiche•173

Italian Wheat Pie•176

Pizza Rustica•179

Sweet Ricotta Pie•183

Cherry on Top•187

Caramel Sauce•189

Bourbon Sauce•190

Hot Fudge Sauce•191

Raspberry Jam•192

Whipped Cream•193

Chocolate Whipped Cream•193

Fluff Whipped Cream•193

Kahlúa Whipped Cream•194

Maple Whipped Cream•194

Acknowledgments•195

Index•197

Some of the many first place ribbons won at National Pie Championships

Introduction

When I opened the first Michele's Pies in December 2007, my goal was simple: to create a space where I could surround myself with the things I love most. Pies filled with the freshest, most flavorful ingredients from local farms and markets. The aroma of apples and cinnamon permeating the air; the feeling of my hands immersed in dough as I knead the perfect crust; customers happily chattering as they select their pies from my shop's display case.

In a little more than four years Michele's Pies has won a total of twenty-six National Pie Championships Awards in the commercial division, and I have won two more (and three honorable mentions) independently in the professional division in categories that include apple, berry, cream, nut, and sugar free. People always want to know the secret to my award-winning pies, and I tell them, "They're made by hand with love." And, although this may sound trite, it's true.

My earliest childhood memories center around my grandma's kitchen, where she and I would spend hours on end peeling fruit, crimping dough, creating glazes, and carefully monitoring our creations to make sure they achieved perfect golden, flaky crusts. At first she would make the pies as I looked on. As time went by, I began to help her, adding flour under her watchful eye, tossing dough, and creating fruit fillings to go into her delicate crusts. For years I carefully observed her pie-making process, until, at last, I could make her pie recipes on my own. This was much easier said than done; my grandma didn't believe in following recipes—she preferred to feel (or, rather, taste) her way through a recipe.

After high school I was convinced that culinary school was for me. My parents, however, placed a strong emphasis on academics and believed a more traditional college education would be a better option. So while I started off on that intended path, life took on a direction of its own after graduation, and I embarked on a career as a nuclear medicine technician at New York City's Mount Sinai Hospital. Although a standard nine-to-five routine set in, pies remained an integral part of my life. I never stopped making them, but they became a personal hobby rather than the professional endeavor I had once dreamed about. Still, after a long day of work at the hospital, I would escape to my home kitchen and lose myself in the comforting smells and rituals of pie making.

As is always the case, however, some surprises were in store for me. In 2000 my beloved mother passed away unexpectedly, and soon thereafter, I found myself back in my Connecticut hometown, caring for my widowed grandma, much as she had cared for me when I was a child. Once back in Connecticut, I made my first career shift, trading in my medical career for a job as a real estate agent. Though I wasn't passionate about the job, it allowed me the opportunity to be near to and care for my grandma. As we had during my childhood, the two of us spent a lot of time in the kitchen, making pies together.

When my grandma passed in 2006, the last thing I said to her was, "Grandma, one day I am going to make your pies famous!" About that same time—one afternoon in April—I happened to turn on a television program about America's top ten pie companies and how many of them had started at local farmers' markets. An entrepreneurial spirit stirred within me. "I can do that!" I thought. Inspired, I immediately began researching and making phone calls, determined to find out exactly how I too could sell my pies at farmers' markets. Unfortunately, I soon learned that Connecticut state laws would require me to work from a commercial kitchen—not a financially feasible scenario.

After a little bit of wallowing, a new thought occurred to me: Just because I couldn't sell my pies in Connecticut didn't mean that I couldn't sell them somewhere else. My ski condo in Killington, Vermont, came to mind—maybe I could run my business from there. With just a few more phone calls, I learned that the laws in Vermont were much less stringent and would allow me to start a pie company right from the comfort of my own home kitchen. I was in business!

Within a week, I found myself in a tiny kitchen in Vermont, surrounded by commercial-size bags of flour, bushels of apples, and crates of berries. Soon I was frequenting the farmers' markets and crafts fairs throughout the state, my pies in tow. Just a few months later, I took my business interstate, attending fall crafts shows and festivals in Connecticut. By the holidays, I was making deliveries throughout Vermont, Connecticut, and New York. It was a crazy and chaotic time, baking the hundreds of pies it took to fill these orders in my own kitchen and then delivering them myself, but it felt great.

Another stroke of luck came a little bit later, when a neighbor told me about her relative who lived in upstate New York and who would be a perfect romantic match for me. Although he was working in the refrigeration industry, he too had the dream of one day opening a bakery. I remember thinking that she was crazy: With my business starting to take off and a heavy workload, how could I possibly contemplate embarking on a long-distance relationship? Nonetheless, I ended up meeting the man who is now my husband and business partner, Kelly.

In fall 2006 the Food Network featured the National Pie Championships—an event I was completely unaware of up to that point. "I can do that!" I once again thought. Just a few months later, I walked away with first place in the commercial nut category of the 2007 competition for my Chocolate-Pecan-Bourbon Pie (page 83). Now, with national recognition under my belt, Kelly convinced me it was time to expand beyond my tiny Vermont ski condo kitchen and open a pie shop. Together, we started looking for commercial spaces in Connecticut and found the perfect space in Norwalk. Michele's Pies was born.

When we first opened the shop in December 2007, I remember thinking how humongous the space was and wondering how we could ever fill up all that room. Well, luck was on my side once again. With very little advertising, word of mouth about the shop spread quickly, helped along by a surprise review of the shop in *The New York Times*. Then, in April 2008, I participated in the National Pie Championships once again, this time taking home four first-place awards.

Adding to the buzz, some of my customers nominated my Chocolate-Pecan-Bourbon Pie as a contender for *Good Morning America*'s Best Pie in America: Best Slice Challenge. I was completely unaware of this until I received a call from a *GMA* producer in November 2008, informing me that I was one of four national finalists. Although the award ultimately went to another baker, my shop had gone national— just a few weeks before Thanksgiving. Michele's Pies was slammed with orders, and my small staff and I worked all hours to fill them as the line of customers spilled outside and snaked all the way around our building.

Seven more first-place awards at the 2009 National Pie Championships preceeded an invitation to be on a Food Network Thanksgiving special that fall. Although I was told it was for a miscellaneous Thanksgiving program, I suspected that I was about to be tossed into the ring for one of Bobby Flay's famous "throwdowns." And, sure enough, when the day arrived, I found myself taping for *Throwdown! with Bobby Flay,* as the two of us made competing versions of my Maple Pumpkin Pie with Pecan Streusel (page 62). Though Bobby (to his own surprise) ultimately won the throwdown, it was truly satisfying to see his eyes light up when he tried my pie. He wrote about our episode in his *Throwdown!* cookbook. "I was pleased with the win but I still have to say that Michele's pie was one of the best pumpkin pies I have ever eaten. It has everything that I look for in a dessert—a creamy texture, big bold balanced flavors and a great contrast of textures." For a second Thanksgiving in a row, customers jammed into Michele's Pies to take home a sampling of our now-famous pumpkin pie to their own holiday tables.

In March 2011, I opened a second Michele's Pies location in Westport, Connecticut, just a few miles away from my flagship Norwalk shop. As I write this I think back on how daunting it was to go into business in the first place and it seems almost impossible to believe that just three and a half years later I own not just one, but two thriving shops.

For all of the unbelievable experiences I've had since Michele's Pies opened for business, it's the day-to-day routine that most satisfies me. Every day when I open the shop's doors and catch a whiff of the sweet and spicy flavors that greet me, I still get a little thrill. I get to spend my days making my favorite pies, creating new ones, and chatting with our customers. Buying pies makes people happy. Pies are a tasty treat, but, more than that, like me, people associate their favorite pies with happy memories and warm holiday celebrations.

What I've also learned from my customers is that the actual process of making pies is often intimidating to them. I always tell them that pies are actually not that difficult to make, and the biggest trick is to always incorporate fresh, local (whenever possible) fruit. Even the dreaded crust—the element of pie making that throws most people off before they even begin—does not have to be daunting. As you read on, you'll find that following just a few simple step-by-step instructions can result in a perfect, flaky, golden brown crust. After all, I have to make hundreds of these crusts myself every day. I don't have time for overly complex, fussy recipes.

The recipes in this book have been categorized according to their level of intricacy. (Note: Intricacy does not necessarily equate with difficulty; some pies simply take more time and require more steps than others.) This organization will help ensure that you never find yourself in a situation where you have only an hour to spend in the kitchen, but are still immersed in the baking process an hour and a half later. Each recipe has one of the following designations:

Easy: 1 hour or less prep time
Moderate: 1 to 2 hours prep time
Challenging: 2 hours or more prep time

Please note that the above times are prep time only: *Baking time is not included.* Generally speaking, allow an additional 45 minutes to 1 hour for baking.

One final bit of advice: Always lay out all of your ingredients before you begin baking. Not only does it save the time and stress of scampering around the kitchen while things are already going, but there's also nothing worse than getting halfway through a recipe and realizing you're missing an essential ingredient.

Although today I am a professional pie maker, I started off just like you: in a home kitchen. Since many of my recipes are derived from the favorite pies my grandma made and my own creations from my early days in that Vermont kitchen, my pies are, by nature, created with the home cook in mind. All of the recipes in this book require no more than your average kitchen tools (see pages xvi–xix) for some of my favorites).

While the excitement in my shop invigorates me, I know what a relaxing, rewarding, and bonding experience making pies in your own kitchen with and for your loved ones can be. After all, the best pies are always made by hand with love.

Kitchen Tools

When it comes to making pies, no fancy tools are required. An American staple, pies were around long before all this specialized cooking equipment. The best pies are the ones that keep it simple, so most of the recipes in this book require you to have no more than measuring utensils, a pie plate, rolling pin, pastry blender, and pastry brush.

The Basics

Measuring cups are used for measuring out dry ingredients and are essential for precision—a primary quality of all perfect pies. I recommend a four- or five-piece set of metal cups (ranging from ¼ cup to 1 cup) as these are the easiest with which to "scoop and sweep." Scooping and sweeping ensures that your measurements are accurate—just dip the appropriate measuring cup into the ingredient, then sweep any excess ingredient off the top with a flat utensil, such as a spatula or knife. **Adjustable measuring cups** are optional, but they also come in handy, particularly when dealing with messy ingredients such as Crisco and peanut butter. These adjustable, all-in-one measuring devices allow for accurate measurements and convenient cleanup—simply discard unused ingredients when you're finished.

Pastry blenders are handheld, curved, wire devices that help incorporate butter into dry ingredients, combining them to create a light, flaky-textured dough by cutting the butter into the flour. The ideal pastry blender is sturdy, has a comfortable grip, sharp blades, is easy-to-use, and doesn't clog. Stainless steel varieties are a favorite because they're dishwasher safe.

Pastry brushes are most frequently used to put the final finish of heavy cream or an egg wash on your crust to ensure an even golden brown color and sheen. Ideally, you want a brush that's not too stiff and that lends itself to a thorough and uniform coating process. Nylon brushes are often on the stiff side. Natural bristle brushes, on the other hand, are nice and pliable and make for smooth spreading. I prefer silicone brushes—they're dishwasher safe and lack the bristles that could come off while brushing and attach themselves to your pastry.

Pie plates used in these recipes are generally the standard 9-inch variety, with the exception of some recipes in the Savory Pies chapter (page 151), which call for a 10-inch deep-dish plate. Pie plates can be found anywhere from the equipment aisle of your local grocery store to specialty cookware stores and come in a number of different materials, ranging from aluminum to steel, glass, and ceramic. In the shop, we use disposable aluminum pie plates so customers can take them home; when baking at home, I use Pyrex glass pie plates. I like glass bottoms because they allow me to examine the bottom crust and ensure it's cooked through all the way. Ceramic pie plates are more difficult to bake with because they can create an uneven finish on the bottom crust and make it difficult to determine whether the bottom crust has fully baked. A commercial-grade, metal-based pie plate will distribute heat more evenly and quickly, making for more efficient and uniform baking results. I prefer a darker finish because it reflects less of the oven heat and helps cook the pie more quickly and evenly. Also, these thicker, higher-quality pie plates tend to be more resistant to scratches and rust and will stand the test of time.

Pie weights are necessary when you're making a pie that requires a pre- or partially baked shell (see page 6). In these instances it's crucial to place something on top of the crust that will allow the crust to keep its form and to stop air bubbles from forming during the early baking process. Pie weights are small balls that come in both metal and ceramic form (I prefer ceramic because they're more hygienic than metal pie weights). As an alternative, you can also use dried beans to hold down the crust—just be aware that beans will begin to crack and break down after several uses.

Rolling pins should have two primary qualities: They should have enough weight that they will roll out dough easily and they should be stick resistant (in other words, they won't take the dough along with them). I prefer rolling pins with handles because they provide more control and require less effort. Rolling rods—or French rolling pins—don't have handles, requiring you to place your palms directly on the rod to apply forward motion and making for a more difficult rolling process. As with pie plates, you can find rolling pins made of a variety of materials, including wood, marble, steel, and glass. I prefer marble rolling pins because they pack a lot of heft, which makes rolling easier, and, on top of that, the coolness of the marble prevents the dough from warming too much. The cooler the dough remains, the less it will break down, which ultimately optimizes the flakiness of the crust.

The Extras

Baking sheets placed directly under pie plates during the baking process will catch any spillage and make the pie easier to take in and out of the oven. Any type of baking sheet will do, but I prefer nonstick varieties, simply because they're easier to clean.

Coarse hand graters are used to zest citrus fruits. I prefer the Microplane Premium Classic Zester/Grater (www.us.miropolane.com) because its long, narrow shape is comfortable to hold, the grater creates a very fine zest, and the tool itself is easily cleaned.

Food processors are used in a handful of the recipes in this book—most notably the various pumpkin pie recipes. I favor Cuisinart brand food processors because I have found them to be the most durable and efficient.

Handheld juicers come in handy if you choose recipes that require a lot of juicing (such as Lemon Meringue Pie, page 39; Twisted Citrus Blackberry Pie, page 127; and Sweet Ricotta Pie, page 183), and will spare you a ton of time and effort.

Kitchen torches are rarely used (unless you make brûlée on a frequent basis), but are helpful to have around if you enjoy making Lemon Meringue Pie (page 39). These handheld devices are great for creating a controlled, evenly browned, caramelized effect on meringue toppings. Kitchen torches can be found at specialty cookware stores. I prefer torches with an adjustable flame because they offer a bit more control when finishing off your pie topping.

Offset spatulas are helpful tools for decorating and adding a finished look to whipped cream–covered pies, such as Candyland Pie (page 137). The thin, flat metal blade is great for spreading the whipped cream and creating a lovely presentation.

Pastry bags allow you to finesse your pies with more decorative cream toppings. There are a ton of different varieties out there, but I prefer Wilton's Featherweight 12-inch decorating bag (www.wilton.com). It doesn't slip, which makes it easy to use (and clean) and gives you a lot of control. You will also need an assortment of pastry tips to use with your pastry bag. I recommend experimenting with tips of different shapes and sizes, all of which result in unique decorating styles. Packages of up to twenty-eight different tips can be found at local cookware retailers and online.

Basic Ingredients

The following ingredients are used frequently throughout the recipes in this book. While all of them are standard items that can be found in your local grocery store, these tips are intended to help you make the best selections and optimally utilize these common ingredients.

Butter is called for in pretty much every recipe here. Feel free to use your favorite brand, but be sure to follow the recipes carefully—some call for unsalted butter and others call for salted butter. Generally speaking, recipes that call for adding salt will use unsalted butter, while those that don't include adding salt will use salted butter.

Crisco is the foundation of a really flaky crust that melts in your mouth. Some people are averse to this shortening because it has a bad reputation for containing trans fats. Rest assured, this is no longer the case. All varieties of modern-day Crisco are trans fat free. Crisco can be messy to work with, but an adjustable measuring cup (see page xvi) will take care of that.

Flour also comes in a variety of brands, but I prefer King Arthur's unbleached all-purpose flour because its high-quality blend of hard and soft wheat creates a slightly more tender, flaky piecrust than other varieties. You should be able to find King Arthur flours at your local grocery store, but, if not, use your favorite brand of unbleached all-purpose flour.

Milk is found frequently in pie recipes. I always use whole milk because it's the most flavorful and has the thickest consistency, which makes for creamier pies. While you can also use lowfat or fat-free milk if you prefer to use slightly less fat, you *will* lose a bit of this creaminess, which is particularly noticeable in cream pie recipes.

Pure Vanilla extract has a much more pure vanilla taste than imitation vanilla flavoring (which is actually made from clove oil). I recommend using 100 percent pure vanilla extract whenever possible. When purchasing vanilla extract, check the ingredients for Madagascar vanilla, which has the highest vanillin concentration, and thus, the strongest vanilla taste.

perfect pies

1

crusts and toppings

....

There's no doubt about it, a light, flaky crust is what sets a good pie apart from a *great* pie. And, at least for me, there are few greater pleasures in life than the perfect slice of pie. Crust is the foundation of it all, and no matter how flavorful and juicy a filling is, without a great crust to complement it, you'll never have the perfect pie.

That said, it probably won't come as much of a surprise that friends and customers often tell me they don't make their own pies because they "just can't get the crust right." Trust me, I'm all for customers coming to my shop as often as possible, but I absolutely guarantee that there's no reason you or they can't create the perfect crust right in the comfort of your own kitchen.

In this chapter you'll find our tried-and-true crust and topping recipes. Over the years I've tweaked and adjusted them to ensure that they're not only straightforward and user friendly, but also that they result in the most delicious crusts possible. Here you'll find classic crust and topping recipes, such as Traditional Pastry Piecrust (page 5) and Cinnamon Sugar Crumb Topping (page 12), as well as more unique options, such as Oreo Cookie Crust (page 11) and Macadamia-Coconut Crumb Topping (page 13).

Before we begin, let's clarify two important terms you'll encounter in this chapter:

Pie shell The pie shell is the bottom crust of your pie, the part that will cover the bottom and sides of your pie plate.

Pie topping/Top crust The pie topping or top crust covers the pie filling and may consist of either a Traditional Pastry Piecrust or a crumb topping, depending on your taste preferences.

In the chapters that follow this, you'll find suggestions for the perfect crust to use with each pie. But feel free to experiment a bit, mixing and matching different pie flavors with different crusts and toppings. It's a great way to consistently enjoy a variety of flavor combinations, cater to your guests' specific taste preferences, and keep things fresh. Most of the experimentation will come in with pie toppings—generally, most recipes in this book use the Traditional Pastry Piecrust, even when some sort of crumb topping is incorporated.

Remember, some pies require that pie shells are baked ahead of time, while others will call for an unbaked crust that's cooked along with the actual pie. Just follow the specific instructions and you'll be making your own perfect piecrusts in no time at all.

Traditional Pastry Piecrust

In my family my grandmother set the bar very high for the perfect, flaky piecrust. Throughout my childhood, I watched her deftly form balls of dough and then flatten them out into what would ultimately be a flawless, golden crust. This recipe is based on my grandma's time-tested recipe, with a few minor alterations I've made over the years. The two biggest tricks to making a great crust are to not overhandle the dough and to carefully monitor the dough mixture as you add ice-cold water, to ensure you achieve the desired consistency. I prefer to make crust by hand, rather than using a food processor because a processor can overblend the shortening which can prevent the water from being evenly absorbed. The result is a tougher crust. Throughout this book, recipes will call for unbaked, prebaked, and partially baked piecrusts, but all will follow the recipe below, with varying specific cooking instructions.

➤ Makes enough for one 9- or 10-inch double crust piecrusts

2 cups unbleached all-purpose flour
1 teaspoon salt
¾ cup plus 2 tablespoons Crisco, cold
5 tablespoons ice-cold water
½ cup heavy cream

In a medium bowl, mix together the flour and the salt. Add the Crisco to the flour mixture. Either with a pastry blender (see page xvi) or with your fingertips, mix the ingredients together with an up-and-down chopping motion until the dough forms coarse, pea-size crumbs. Note: I prefer the old-fashioned fingertip option, but take care not to overhandle the dough, because it will become difficult to work with—when dough is overhandled, the Crisco becomes *too* incorporated. In the perfect pie, the Crisco will have a marbleized look, and you will actually be able to see Crisco swirls within the uncooked dough.

Add the ice-cold water, 1 tablespoon at a time, delicately incorporating each tablespoon into the flour mixture before you add the next. You may have to use 1 more or 1 less tablespoon of water than the amount recommended, depending upon the humidity in your kitchen at the time of baking. You will know you have added just the right amount of water when the dough forms a ball that easily holds together.

Wrap the ball of dough with plastic and place it in the refrigerator to chill for at least 30 minutes. Once the dough has chilled, divide the ball in half. You now have enough dough for either one 9- or 10-inch double crust (1 pie shell and 1 top crust) or two 9- or 10-inch single crusts (pie shell only). If you are making a single-crust pie, you will use only one half of the dough per pie. Wrap the remaining half in plastic and reserve it in the refrigerator for future use; the dough can be reserved in the refrigerator for up to 5 days. Alternatively, you can make a second single-crust pie, wrap it tightly in plastic wrap, and freeze it for future use; it will keep for up to 1 month.

Preparing prebaked and partially baked pie shells

A number of recipes in this book call for prebaked or partially baked pie shells for the single crust pies. Follow these directions before adding desired filling.

Preheat the oven to 425°F.

To prepare the pie shell, divide the ball of dough in half, setting one half to the side. On a clean, lightly floured work surface, roll out the dough with a rolling pin until it forms a 10-inch circle. Fold the circle in half, place it in the pie plate so the edges of the circle drop over the rim, and unfold the dough to completely cover the pie plate. Crimp the edges of the pie shell by using the index finger of one hand to push the inner edge of the crust out, while using the thumb and index finger of your other hand to push the outer edge in. Brush heavy cream over the crimped edges to create a perfect, golden brown finish. Line the bottom of the crust with parchment paper and place pie weights (see page xvii) on top to ensure the edges do not fall into the shell while the crust is baking.

For prebaked pie shells, bake the crust at 425°F on the middle rack of the oven (see page 24) for 15 to 20 minutes, or until a golden brown color is achieved. Before removing the shell from the oven, make sure that the crust under the parchment paper has turned a golden brown.

For partially baked pie shells, follow the instructions as outlined above, but bake the pie shell for only 10 minutes so the crust only just begins to bake. (Note: Partially baked pie shells will be used for pies that have quick-bake fillings, such as Key Lime Pie, page 120.)

Using Cold Ingredients for Crusts and Toppings

· · · · · · · · · · · · · · · · · · ·

When making crusts and toppings, it's important that the Crisco, butter, and water are cold at the time of preparation. A flaky crust texture is created when shortening and butter remain cool enough that they don't melt into the other ingredients throughout the preparation process. Put ice cubes in the water to ensure that it's as cold as possible; Crisco and butter should be refrigerated prior to use.

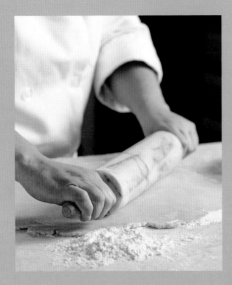

Roll out the dough until about ⅛ inch thick.
Make a circle about 10 inches in diameter.

Fold the dough circle in half so that it can easily
be lifted and place over the pie dish.

Unfold the dough until the dish is completely covered, then gently pat the dough into the pie dish so that
it fits snugly. If dough tears, gently pinch together with fingertips.

To crimp the pie dough, use your forefingers and thumbs. Press down with your forefingers and up with your thumbs to crimp the dough. Continue to crimp until the entire pie is completed.

Using
Pie Weights

• • • • • • • • • • • •

When using pie weights, cut a piece of parchment paper into a square shape and place it on top of the pie shell. Next, place the pie weights (see page xvii)—distributing them evenly—on top of the parchment paper.

Graham Cracker Crust

Extremely simple to make, this crust infuses pies with an unexpected sweet honey taste and a great, crunchy texture. It pairs especially well with Twisted Citrus Blackberry Pie (page 127), S'more's Delight Pie (page 145), and Banana Cream Pie (page 109). You can also keep it simple and fill this crust with a vanilla pastry cream filling (which can be found as part of the Boston Cream Pie recipe on page 99), then top it with Whipped Cream (page 193) or Meringue (see page 39).

▶ Makes one 9-inch crust

24 graham cracker sheets, finely chopped (1½ cups)
 1 tablespoon sugar
 5 tablespoons unsalted butter, melted

Preheat the oven to 350°F.

In a medium bowl, mix together the graham cracker crumbs and sugar. Add the melted butter, using your fingertips to incorporate it with the graham cracker mixture. Spread the graham cracker mixture evenly across the bottom and sides of a 9-inch pie plate so that it covers the entire dish. There should be no gaps in the crust. Bake the crust for about 5 minutes, or until it's golden brown. Cool the pie shell for 30 minutes before adding your desired filling.

Oreo Cookie Crust

Talk about having your cookie and eating it, too! Be sure to try this crust with classic Chocolate Cream Pie (page 102), Coffee–Heath Bar Crunch Pie (page 118), Chocolate–Peanut Butter Dream Pie (page 104), and Candyland Pie (page 137). For an especially simple treat, you can fill this crust with vanilla ice cream—it's the easiest ice cream pie you could ever hope for.

▶ Makes one 9-inch crust

1½ cups Oreo cookie crumbs (approximately 20 Oreo cookies)
½ teaspoon ground cinnamon
2 tablespoons unsalted butter, melted
2 tablespoons whole milk

Preheat the oven to 350°F.

Place the Oreo cookies and cinnamon in a food processor (see page xviii) and pulse them together until they are ground down into fine crumbs. In a medium bowl, mix together the crumbs and melted butter, using a fork to combine. Add and incorporate the milk, ½ tablespoon at a time, stopping when the crumbs are moist enough to mold into a pie shell (this may take only 1½ tablespoons of milk to accomplish).

Spread the Oreo crust mixture evenly across the bottom and sides of a 9-inch pie plate so that it covers the entire dish. There should be no gaps in the crust. Bake for 5 minutes. Cool the pie shell for 30 minutes before adding your desired pie filling.

Cinnamon Sugar Crumb Topping

If your family has a favorite kind of fruit pie, this traditional crumb topping is a great way to mix things up on top while keeping the Traditional Pastry Piecrust (page 5) on the bottom. It adds a sweetness and texture that blend wonderfully with a number of fruit pies, including Country Apple Pie (page 19), Blueberry Pie (page 27), and Peach Crumb Pie (page 43), to name just a few. This crumb topping can be made ahead of time and kept in the refrigerator for up to five days before use.

➤ Makes enough topping for one 9-inch pie

½ cup unbleached all-purpose flour
⅓ cup firmly packed light brown sugar
1 teaspoon ground cinnamon
¼ teaspoon salt
5 tablespoons unsalted butter, cold and cut into ¼-inch cubes

In a large bowl, mix together the flour, brown sugar, cinnamon, and salt. Using a pastry blender, incorporate the butter by "cutting it in" to the flour until the butter forms small, pea-size pieces.

Pair this topping with a traditional pastry pie shell and the filling of your choice. Once the filling has been placed in the pie shell, sprinkle the cinnamon sugar crumb topping evenly over the filling until it is completely covered. Bake as directed.

Macadamia-Coconut Crumb Topping

This is not your average pie topping. Macadamia-Coconut Crumb screams "summertime," adding a refreshing tropical twist to even the most classic pie recipes. This topping really enhances pineapple- and mango-based pies (see Pineapple-Mango Pie, page 57), but works well with any tropical fruit pie recipe. It will also transform Peach Crumb Pie (page 43) or Blueberry Pie (page 27) into an extra special dessert.

▶ Makes enough topping for one 9-inch pie

½ cup unbleached all-purpose flour
⅓ cup firmly packed light brown sugar
1 teaspoon ground cinnamon
¼ teaspoon salt
5 tablespoons unsalted butter, cold and cut into ¼-inch cubes
¼ cup sweetened shredded coconut
½ cup finely chopped macadamia nuts

In a large bowl, mix together the flour, brown sugar, cinnamon, and salt. Using a pastry blender, incorporate the butter by "cutting it in" to the flour until the buter forms small, pea-size pieces. Add the coconut and macadamia nuts, and mix with the pastry blender until all of the ingredients are well combined.

Pair this topping with a traditional pastry pie shell and the filling of your choice. Once the filling has been placed in the pie shell, distribute the macadamia-coconut crumb topping evenly over the filling until it is completely covered. Bake as directed.

Walnut Crumb Topping

This topping uses the same base as the Cinnamon Sugar Crumb Topping (page 12), but adds walnuts to the mix, providing an added bit of crunch. Feel free to experiment with this recipe according to your nut preferences—walnuts can easily be swapped out for pecans, hazelnuts, or any other nut that suits your fancy. This topping is ideal for Pear Cranberry Pie (page 53).

▶ Makes enough topping for one 9-inch pie

½ cup unbleached all-purpose flour
⅔ cup firmly packed light brown sugar
1½ teaspoons ground cinnamon
¼ teaspoon salt
5 tablespoons unsalted butter, cold and cut into ¼-inch cubes
¼ cup chopped walnuts

In a large bowl, combine the flour, brown sugar, cinnamon, and salt. Using a pastry blender, incorporate the butter by "cutting it in" to the flour until the butter forms small, pea-size pieces. Add in the chopped walnuts, using your fingers to gently incorporate them into the crumb base.

Pair this topping with a traditional pastry pie shell and the filling of your choice. Once the filling has been placed in the pie shell, distribute the walnut crumb topping evenly over the filling until it is completely covered. Bake as directed.

2

farm stand pies

It comes as no surprise that some of the most beloved classic pies are fruit pies—it's hard to beat the combination of fresh fruit juices intermingling with a flaky pastry crust. Country Apple Pie (page 19), Pumpkin Pie (page 59), Peach Crumb Pie (page 43)—not only have we all had them, but many of these are actually an integral part of our holiday meals and seasonal traditions.

For me, fruit pies are particularly gratifying to make because they allow me to hunt down the best, freshest seasonal ingredients and immediately put them to good use. In the summertime, you'll find me on the lookout for the juiciest raspberries and cherries Connecticut has to offer. In fall, I'm gathering bins of sugar pumpkins from the local Jones Family Farms for our award-winning Pumpkin Pie. When people ask me what the secret to my pies is, I often tell them that it's the fact they're "made by hand with love." While this is certainly true, another big secret to my success is that I *always* use fresh fruit, never frozen or canned. So for the best results, I urge you to use fresh, in-season local fruits whenever possible.

Have fun with these fruit pies and be sure to mix it up. Some fruit pie recipes will provide suggestions for alternate crusts and toppings, but you should also feel free to come up with your own creations as well.

Country Apple Pie

Apple pie seems like the perfect place to begin, since it was the first pie I ever made. Despite all of the practice I had making this pie as a kid with my grandma, it took me a very long time to commit this recipe to paper; but, after many tries, I was finally able to get her recipe down! Select your apples based on your own taste preferences. At the shop, we use Cortland apples for their sweetness (Fuji, Gala, Golden Delicious, Honey Crisp or McIntosh are also sweet). You can also get creative and use a combination of both sweet and tart apples, such as Fuji and Granny Smith apples (Jonathan and Rome Beauties are tart as well). You can also try this pie with the Cinnamon Sugar Crumb Topping (page 12) and drizzled with Caramel Sauce (page 189); it earned us two National Pie Championships Award.

▶ level: easy   Makes one 9-inch pie, 6 to 8 slices

Crust

1 recipe Traditional Pastry Piecrust dough for a 9-inch double-crust pie (page 5)

½ cup heavy cream (to glaze the top crust and crimped pie edges)

Filling

¾ cup sugar

2 tablespoons unbleached all-purpose flour

1 tablespoon ground cinnamon

Dash of ground nutmeg

8 medium apples, peeled, cored, and cut into ½-inch chunks

1 tablespoon salted butter

Preheat the oven to 425°F.

To prepare the pie shell, divide the ball of dough in half, setting one half to the side. On a clean, lightly floured work surface, roll out the dough with a rolling pin

until it forms a 10-inch circle. Fold the circle in half, place it in a 9-inch pie plate so that the edges of the circle drop over the rim, and unfold the dough to completely cover the pie plate. Set the pie shell to the side while you make the filling.

To prepare the filling, in a small bowl, whisk together the sugar, flour, cinnamon, and nutmeg. Place the apples in a large bowl and sprinkle them with the sugar mixture, making sure the apples are thoroughly coated. Place the apple mixture in the pie shell, distributing it evenly. Dot the filling with the butter.

To prepare the top crust, roll out the second half of dough with a rolling pin until it forms a 10-inch circle. Fold the dough circle in half and place it over the filling, with the straight line of the half circle running down the middle of the pie. Unfold the circle so that the entire pie is covered. Using your thumb and index finger, crimp the edges of the pie together to seal in the filling, and then use a fork to puncture the top of the pie 5 or 6 times. Brush the top of the pie and crimped edges with heavy cream to create a perfect, golden brown finish.

To bake, place the pie plate on a baking sheet and bake for 15 minutes. Reduce the heat to 375°F and continue baking for 40 minutes, or until the apples are tender. Insert a cake tester or a knife into the pie to check the firmness of the apples. If the apples are still firm, continue baking the pie until they soften. The perfect apple pie will have visible juices bubbling around the crust. If the top of the crust is getting too brown and the apples are not done yet, cover the pie with aluminum foil to allow the apples to bake a bit longer without browning the crust too much. Transfer the pie plate to a wire cooling rack and allow the pie to cool and set for 1½ hours before serving.

Apple pies are best served either at room temperature or warmed at 350°F for about 10 minutes. Country Apple Pie will keep at room temperature overnight and can be stored in the refrigerator for up to 4 days.

Apple-Raspberry Pie Variation

Make the filling according to the Country Apple Pie instructions, adding ½ cup fresh raspberries to the apple filling after the sugar mixture has been incorporated. Gently mix in the raspberries. Proceed as directed.

Sugar-Free Apple Pie

Around here, National Pie Day (January 23) is like Christmas, Hanukkah, and Thanksgiving rolled up into one! Every year on this holy pie day, I like to do something special. In 2009 I decided National Pie Day would be the perfect opportunity to roll out a line of sugar-free pies. Incorporating Splenda into the sugar-free pies allows you to undulge in a sweet treat while limiting your sugar intake. Sugar-free apple pies have been flying off the shelves ever since—a great way to savor apple pie minus the guilt.

▶ level: easy Makes one 9-inch pie, 6 to 8 slices

Crust

1 recipe Traditional Pastry Piecrust dough for a 9-inch double-crust pie (page 5)
½ cup heavy cream (to glaze the top crust and crimped pie edges)

Filling

½ cup Splenda No Calorie Sweetener
1 teaspoon ground cinnamon
2 tablespoons unbleached all-purpose flour
½ teaspoon ground nutmeg
8 medium apples, peeled, cored, and cut into ½-inch chunks
1 tablespoon salted butter

Preheat the oven to 425°F.

To prepare the pie shell, divide the ball of dough in half, setting one half to the side. On a clean, lightly floured work surface, roll out the dough with a rolling pin until it forms a 10-inch circle. Fold the circle in half, place it in a 9-inch pie plate so that the edges of the circle drop over the rim, and unfold the dough to completely cover the pie plate. Set the pie shell to the side while you make the filling.

To prepare the filling, in a small bowl, mix together the Splenda, cinnamon, flour, and nutmeg. Place the apples in a large bowl and sprinkle them with the Splenda mixture, making sure all of the apples are thoroughly coated. Place the apple mixture in the pie shell, distributing it evenly. Dot the filling with the butter.

To prepare the top crust, roll out the second half of the dough with a rolling pin until it forms a 10-inch circle. Fold the dough circle in half and place it over the filling, with the straight line of the half circle running down the middle of the pie. Unfold the circle so that the entire pie is covered. Using your thumb and index finger, crimp the edges of the pie together to seal in the filling, and then use a fork to puncture the top of the pie 5 or 6 times. Brush the top of the pie and crimped edges with heavy cream to create a perfect, golden brown finish.

To bake, place the pie plate on a baking sheet and bake for 15 minutes. Reduce the heat to 375°F and continue baking for 40 minutes, or until the apples are tender. Insert a cake tester or a knife into the pie to check the firmness of the apples. If the apples are still firm, continue baking the pie until they soften. The perfect apple pie will have visible juices bubbling around the crust. If the top of the crust is getting too brown and the apples are not done yet, cover the pie with aluminum foil to allow the apples to bake a bit longer without browning the crust too much. Transfer the pie plate to a wire cooling rack and allow the pie to cool and set for 1½ hours before serving.

Apple pies are best served either at room temperature or warmed at 350°F for about 10 minutes. Sugar-Free Apple Pie will keep at room temperature overnight and can be stored in the refrigerator for up to 4 days.

Apple-Cranberry Crumb Pie

Unlike fresh cranberries, which can be tart, dried cranberries provide an extra layer of sweetness to the classic apple pie. This dessert is a great finale to a pork roast dinner. Try it with the Traditional Pastry double crust (page 5) as an alternative.

▶ level: easy   Makes one 9-inch pie, 6 to 8 slices

Crust and Topping

   1   recipe Traditional Pastry Piecrust dough for a single-crust pie (page 5)

  ¼   cup heavy cream (to glaze the crimped pie edges)

      Cinnamon Sugar Crumb Topping (page 12)

Filling

  ¾   cup sugar

   2   tablespoons unbleached all-purpose flour

   1   tablespoon ground cinnamon

     Dash of ground nutmeg

   8   medium apples, peeled, cored, and cut into ½-inch chunks

  ⅔   cup dried cranberries

Preheat the oven to 425°F.

To prepare the pie shell, on a clean, lightly floured work surface, roll out half a ball of dough with a rolling pin until it forms a 10-inch circle. Wrap the remaining half of the dough tightly in plastic wrap and reserve it in the refrigerator for future use for up to 5 days. Fold the circle in half, place it in a 9-inch pie plate so that the edges of the circle drop over the rim, and unfold the dough to completely cover the pie plate. Using your thumb and index finger, crimp the edges of the pie shell. Brush the edges of the pie shell with heavy cream to create a perfect, golden brown finish. Set the pie shell to the side while you make the filling.

To prepare the filling, in a small bowl, whisk together the sugar, flour, cinnamon, and nutmeg. Place the apples in a large bowl and toss them with the sugar mixture, making sure all of the apples are thoroughly coated. Add the dried cranberries, mixing well to ensure they are fully incorporated into the apple mixture. Place the apple mixture in the pie shell, distributing it evenly. Sprinkle the cinnamon-sugar crumb topping over the apple-cranberry filling, covering it completely.

To bake, place the pie plate on a baking sheet and bake for 15 minutes. Reduce the heat to 375°F and continue baking for 40 minutes, or until the apples are tender. Insert a cake tester or a knife into the pie to check the firmness of the apples. If the apples are still firm, continue baking the pie until they soften. The perfect apple pie will have visible juices bubbling around the topping. If the topping is getting too brown and the apples are not done yet, cover the pie with aluminum foil to allow the apples to bake a bit longer without browning the topping too much. Transfer the pie plate to a wire cooling rack and allow the pie to cool and set for 1½ hours before serving.

Apple pies are best served either at room temperature or warmed at 350°F for about 10 minutes. Apple-Cranberry Crumb pie will keep at room temperature overnight and can be stored in the refrigerator for up to 4 days.

Achieving the Perfect Evenly Baked Crust

. . . .

When baking pies, oven racks should be set at mid-level, in the center, during the baking process so that the entire pie bakes through evenly (in other words, to ensure your crust and filling are finished baking at the same time and you don't end up with crispy crust and undercooked filling). Rotating your pies 180 degrees halfway through the cooking time will also help ensure an evenly baked golden brown crust.

Blackberry Pie

My business partner and husband, Kelly, *loves* reminiscing about picking plump, juicy wild blackberries as a child with his grandma at their camp in the Adirondacks. Although Kelly loved eating the blackberries almost as quickly as he could pick them, he knew that if he managed to leave enough, his grandma would make his favorite summer treat—Blackberry Pie. Check out local farms or farmers' markets for access to the sweetest blackberries available in your area. June is usually peak blackberry season in the southern states, while they peak in July up north. You can also try this pie with the Cinnamon Sugar Crumb Topping (page 12).

▶ level: easy   Makes one 9-inch pie, 6 to 8 slices

Crust
- 1 recipe Traditional Pastry Piecrust dough for a 9-inch double-crust pie (page 5)
- ½ cup heavy cream (to glaze the top crust and crimped pie edges)

Filling
- ¾ cup sugar (or to taste, depending on the sweetness of the berries)
- ½ cup unbleached all-purpose flour
- ¾ teaspoon ground cinnamon
- 4 cups blackberries, washed and thoroughly dried
- 1 tablespoon salted butter

Preheat the oven to 400°F.

To prepare the pie shell, on a clean, lightly floured work surface, roll out half of the dough with a rolling pin until it forms a 10-inch circle. Fold the circle in half, place it in the pie plate so the edges of the circle drop over the rim, and unfold the dough to completely cover the pie plate. Set the pie shell to the side while you make the filling.

To prepare the filling, in a small bowl, whisk together the sugar, flour, and cinnamon. Place the blackberries in a large bowl and toss them gently with the sugar mixture, handling the fruit delicately and making sure all of the blackberries are thoroughly coated. Place the blackberries in the pie shell carefully, so as not to break down the berries too much. Dot the filling with the butter.

To prepare the top crust, roll out the second half of dough with a rolling pin until it forms a 10-inch circle. Fold the dough circle in half and place it over the filling, with the straight line of the half circle running down the middle of the pie. Unfold the circle so that the entire pie is covered. Using your thumb and index finger, crimp the edges of the pie together to seal in the filling, and then use a fork to puncture the top of the pie 5 or 6 times. Brush the top of the pie and crimped edges with heavy cream for a perfect, golden brown finish.

To bake, place the pie plate on a baking sheet and bake for 15 minutes. Reduce the heat to 375°F and continue baking for 40 to 45 minutes, or until the crust is browned and the juice bubbles through. Transfer the pie plate to a wire cooling rack and allow the pie to cool and set for 1½ hours before serving.

Blackberry Pie is best served either at room temperature or warmed at 350°F for about 10 minutes. It will keep at room temperature overnight and can be stored in the refrigerator for up to 4 days.

Blueberry Pie

My dad and I have spent a lifetime bonding over our love of blueberry pie. I knew I had mastered this recipe when I got his stamp of approval. When selecting blueberries, remember that they don't sweeten after being picked. Generally, the bigger a blueberry is, the sweeter it is. Try to use big, round berries, without cracked skin, and be sure to pick the stems off the blueberries before using. Summertime is the best time for this pie because the berries are at their prime between June and early September. You can also try Blueberry Pie with the Cinnamon Sugar Crumb Topping (page 12) which won the 2011 National Pie Championships in its category. For extra indulgence add a scoop of vanilla ice cream.

▶ level: easy   Makes one 9-inch pie, 6 to 8 slices

Crust

1   recipe Traditional Pastry Piecrust dough for a 9-inch double-crust pie (page 5)

½   cup heavy cream (to glaze the top crust and crimped pie edges)

Filling

¼   cup plus 2 tablespoons sugar (or to taste, depending on the sweetness of the berries; if they are on the tart side, add the extra sugar, 1 tablespoon at a time, to taste)

⅓   cup plus 2 tablespoons unbleached all-purpose flour

¾   teaspoon ground cinnamon

4   cups fresh blueberries, washed, dried, and stemmed

1   tablespoon fresh lemon juice

1   tablespoon salted butter

Preheat the oven to 425°F.

   To prepare the pie shell, divide the ball of dough in half, setting one half to the

side. On a clean, lightly floured work surface, roll out the dough with a rolling pin until it forms a 10-inch circle. Fold the circle in half, place it in a 9-inch pie plate so that the edges of the circle drop over the rim, and unfold the dough to completely cover the pie plate. Set the pie shell to the side while you assemble the filling.

To prepare the filling, in a small bowl, whisk together the sugar, flour, and cinnamon. Place the blueberries in a large bowl and toss them gently with the sugar mixture, making sure all of the berries are thoroughly coated. Place the blueberry mixture in the pie shell, distributing it evenly. Evenly sprinkle the lemon juice across the top of the berry filling. Dot the filling with the butter.

To prepare the top crust, roll out the second half of the dough with a rolling pin until it forms a 10-inch circle. Fold the dough circle in half and place it over the filling, with the straight line of the half circle running down the middle of the pie. Unfold the circle so that the entire pie is covered. Using your thumb and index finger, crimp the edges of the pie together to seal in the filling, and then use a fork to puncture the top of the pie 5 or 6 times. Brush the top of the pie and crimped edges with heavy cream to create a perfect, golden brown finish.

To bake, place the pie plate on a baking sheet and bake for 15 minutes. Reduce the heat to 375°F and continue baking for 40 to 45 minutes, or until the crust is browned and the juice bubbles through. Transfer the pie plate to a wire cooling rack and allow the pie to cool and set for 1½ hours before serving.

Blueberry Pie is best served either at room temperature or warmed at 350°F for about 10 minutes. It will keep at room temperature overnight and can be stored in the refrigerator for up to 4 days.

Sugar-Free Blueberry Pie

This pie allows for indulgence in a sweet treat. Blueberries pack enough flavor that you'll never even know that traditional sugar is missing.

▶ level: easy   Makes one 9-inch pie, 6 to 8 slices

Crust

1 recipe Traditional Pastry Piecrust dough for a 9-inch double-crust pie (page 5)

½ cup heavy cream (to glaze the top crust and crimped pie edges)

Filling

⅓ cup Splenda

⅓ cup plus 2 tablespoons unbleached all-purpose flour

¾ teaspoon ground cinnamon

4 cups fresh blueberries, washed, dried, and stemmed

1 tablespoon fresh lemon juice

1 tablespoon salted butter

Preheat the oven to 425°F.

To prepare the pie shell, divide the ball of dough in half, setting one half to the side. On a clean, lightly floured work surface, roll out the dough with a rolling pin until it forms a 10-inch circle. Fold the circle in half, place it in the pie plate so the edges of the circle drop over the rim, and unfold the dough to completely cover the pie plate. Set the pie shell to the side while you make the filling.

To prepare the filling, in a small bowl, whisk together the Splenda, flour, and cinnamon. Place the blueberries in a large bowl and toss them gently with the Splenda mixture, making sure all of the berries are thoroughly coated. Place the blueberry mixture in the pie shell, distributing it evenly. Sprinkle the lemon juice across the top of the blueberry filling. Dot the filling with the butter.

To prepare the top crust, roll out the second half of the dough with a rolling pin until it forms a 10-inch circle. Fold the dough circle in half and place it over the filling, with the straight line of the half circle running down the middle of the pie. Unfold the circle so that the entire pie is covered. Using your thumb and index finger, crimp the edges of the pie together to seal in the filling, and then use a fork to puncture the top of the pie 5 or 6 times. Brush the top of the pie and crimped edges with heavy cream to create a perfect, golden brown finish.

To bake, place the pie plate on a baking sheet and bake for 15 minutes. Reduce the heat to 375°F and continue baking for 40 to 45 minutes, or until the crust is browned and the juice bubbles through. Transfer the pie plate to a wire cooling rack and allow the pie to cool and set for 1½ hours before serving.

Sugar-Free Blueberry Pie is best served either at room temperature or warmed at 350°F for about 10 minutes. It will keep at room temperature overnight and can be stored in the refrigerator for up to 4 days.

Why Puncture Pie Top Crusts?

. . . .

Using a fork to puncture 5 or 6 holes in the top crust provides ventilation, allowing steam and moisture to release during the baking process. Though these punctures serve a utilitarian purpose, you can also get creative with puncture patterns. For example, when making an apple pie, I puncture the top crust with an A shape.

Blueberry-Blackberry Crumb Pie

This pie was one of my very first entries in the National Pie Championships. It ended up winning the 2008 Championships in the berry category. The most important element when it comes to a successful result with this pie is to use just picked firm berries. I recommend making Blueberry-Blackberry Pie with a crumb topping; however, if you prefer a less sweet fruit pie, go with the Traditional Pastry double-crust option (page 5), which is just as good. This pie shines with a dollop of Whipped Cream (page 193) or vanilla ice cream.

▶ level: easy   Makes one 9-inch pie, 6 to 8 slices

Crust and Topping

1 recipe Traditional Pastry Piecrust dough for a 9-inch single-crust pie (page 5)

¼ cup heavy cream (to glaze the crimped pie edges)

Cinnamon Sugar Crumb Topping (page 12)

Filling

¾ cup sugar

⅓ cup unbleached all-purpose flour

1 teaspoon ground cinnamon

2 cups fresh blueberries, stemmed, washed, and dried well

2 cups fresh blackberries, washed and dried well

Preheat the oven to 425°F.

To prepare the pie shell, on a clean, lightly floured work surface, roll out half a ball of dough with a rolling pin until it forms a 10-inch circle. Wrap the remaining half of the dough tightly in plastic wrap and reserve it in the refrigerator for future use for up to 5 days. Fold the circle in half, place it in a 9-inch pie plate so that the

edges of the circle drop over the rim, and unfold the dough to completely cover the pie plate. Using your thumb and index finger, crimp the edges of the pie shell. Brush the edges of the pie shell with heavy cream to create a perfect, golden brown finish. Set the pie shell to the side while you make the filling.

To prepare the filling, in a small bowl, whisk together the sugar, flour, and cinnamon. Place the berries in a large bowl and toss them gently with the sugar mixture, making sure all of the berries are thoroughly coated (be careful not to break down the berries while tossing because that will create unwanted juice). Place the berry mixture in the pie shell, distributing it evenly. Sprinkle the cinnamon sugar crumb topping over the blueberry-blackberry filling, covering it completely.

To bake, place the pie plate on a baking sheet and bake for 15 minutes. Reduce the heat to 350°F and continue baking for 40 minutes, or until the crust is golden brown and the juice bubbles over the side. Transfer the pie plate to a wire cooling rack and allow the pie to cool and set for 1½ hours before serving.

Blueberry-Blackberry Crumb Pie is best served either at room temperature or warmed at 350°F for about 10 minutes. It will keep at room temperature overnight and can be stored in the refrigerator for up to 4 days.

Cherry Pie

Our customers look forward to this pie just as much as they look forward to fireworks on the Fourth of July—the perfect holiday for indulging in this pie because late June to early August is when cherries tend to be at their most flavorful. Although this recipe calls for Bing cherries, which are easiest to find, you can substitute whatever is available in your area. A little more prep time is required here than for other fruit pies because of the pitting process, but it's well worth the effort. This recipe uses a lattice-style top crust, but you can also use a traditionally placed top crust if you prefer. You can also try this pie with Cinnamon Sugar Crumb Topping (page 12).

▶ level: moderate   Makes one 9-inch pie, 6 to 8 slices

Crust

1 recipe Traditional Pastry Piecrust dough for a 9-inch double-crust pie (page 5)

½ cup heavy cream (to glaze the top crust and crimped pie edges)

Filling

4½ cups fresh Bing cherries, stemmed, pitted, and halved

½ cup plus 2 tablespoons sugar

2 tablespoons fresh lemon juice

3 tablespoons cornstarch

Pinch of ground nutmeg

Pinch of ground cinnamon

Preheat the oven to 425°F.

To prepare the pie shell, divide the ball of dough in half, setting one half to the side. On a clean, lightly floured work surface, roll out the dough with a rolling pin until it forms a 10-inch circle. Fold the circle in half, place it in a 9-inch pie plate so that the edges of the circle drop over the rim, and unfold the dough to completely cover the pie plate. Set the pie shell to the side while you make the filling.

To prepare the filling, in a large bowl, mix together the cherries, ½ cup sugar, and the lemon juice. Set the bowl aside for approximately 5 minutes, allowing the juice to set. In a small bowl, mix together the remaining 2 tablespoons sugar, the cornstarch, the nutmeg, and the cinnamon. Add the cornstarch mixture to the cherries and mix well. Place the cherry mixture in the pie shell, distributing it evenly.

To prepare the top crust, roll out the second half of the dough with a rolling pin until it forms a 10-inch circle. Using a sharp knife or a pastry wheel, cut the dough circle into ¾-inch strips. Place the strips over the top of the pie filling, lattice style, so that the edges of each strip meet the crimped edges of the bottom crust. Ultimately, you want to create a checkerboard effect, with the lattice strips placed both vertically and horizontally across the pie. Brush the crust edges and lattice strips with heavy cream for a perfect, golden brown finish.

To bake, place the pie plate on a baking sheet and bake for 15 minutes. Reduce the heat to 375°F and continue baking for 35 to 40 minutes, or until the crust is golden brown and the juices begin to bubble. Transfer the pie plate to a wire cooling rack and allow the pie to cool and set for 1½ hours before serving.

Cherry Pie is best served either at room temperature or warmed at 350°F for about 10 minutes. It will keep at room temperature overnight and can be stored in the refrigerator for up to 4 days.

Roll out a 10-inch circle on your surface. With a pastry wheel, cut 1-inch thick pieces so that you have 5 pieces.

Place the pieces horizontally on top of your filling. Then roll out another 10-inch circle. Cut again 1-inch thick pieces so that you have 5 pieces.

Take one piece at a time and weave the pieces in and out of the horizontal pieces. Do this until the entire pie has been completed.

Trim off excess pieces and crimp lattice strips to pie crust.

Sour Cherry Crunch Pie

Since the majority of sour cherry patches are in Michigan, Utah, and Washington State, depending on where you live, you may be unaware of these ruby-red delicacies. It's worth hunting them down—just be aware that they are very perishable and should be frozen immediately or put straight to use in this scrumptious pie. For a little bit of added texture, I like to use this walnut crunch topping, infused with a bit of orange zest for that extra zing.

▶ level: moderate   Makes one 9-inch pie, 6 to 8 slices

Crust
1 recipe Traditional Pastry Piecrust dough for a 9-inch single-crust pie (page 5)

¼ cup heavy cream (to glaze the crimped pie edges)

Filling
1 cup granulated sugar

¼ teaspoon salt

3 tablespoons cornstarch

5 cups sour cherries, stemmed, pitted, and drained

1½ teaspoons fresh lemon juice

1 teaspoon pure vanilla extract

Crunch Topping
½ cup unbleached all-purpose flour

⅓ cup firmly packed light brown sugar

Zest of ½ orange

¾ cup coarsely chopped walnuts

1 teaspoon ground cinnamon

¼ teaspoon salt

5 tablespoons unsalted butter, cold and cut into ¼-inch cubes

Preheat the oven to 425°F.

To prepare the pie shell, on a clean, lightly floured work surface, roll out half a ball of dough with a rolling pin until it forms a 10-inch circle. Wrap the remaining half of the dough tightly in plastic wrap and reserve it in the refrigerator for future use for up to 5 days. Fold the circle in half, place it in a 9-inch pie plate so that the edges of the circle drop over the rim, and unfold the dough to completely cover the pie plate. Using your thumb and index finger, crimp the edges of the pie shell. Brush the edges of the pie shell with heavy cream to create a perfect, golden brown finish. Set the pie shell to the side while you make the filling.

To prepare the filling, in a medium bowl, whisk together the granulated sugar, salt, and cornstarch. Add the sour cherries, and toss them gently with the sugar mixture, making sure all of the berries are thoroughly coated. Stir in the lemon juice and vanilla. Place the cherry filling in the pie shell, distributing it evenly.

To prepare the crunch topping, in a medium bowl, using a pastry blender, combine the flour, brown sugar, orange zest, walnuts, cinnamon, and salt. Using a pastry blender, incorporate the butter until pea-size pieces form. Sprinkle the topping over the cherry filling, covering it completely.

To bake, place the pie plate on a baking sheet and bake for 15 minutes. Reduce the heat to 375°F and continue baking for 45 minutes, or until the crunch topping has achieved a golden brown color and the cherry juices are bubbling. Transfer the pie plate to a wire cooling rack and allow the pie to cool and set for 1½ hours before serving.

Sour Cherry Crunch Pie is best served either at room temperature or warmed at 350°F for about 10 minutes. It will keep at room temperature overnight and can be stored in the refrigerator for up to 4 days.

Lemon Meringue Pie

As if the bold, tart flavor weren't appealing enough, this pie is absolutely beautiful to behold. A mound of fluffy white meringue, toasted on top and offset by the rich yellow of the lemon curd, makes for a picture-perfect slice of pie. Best served the same day it is made, you can make the lemon curd in advance and refrigerate it in the pie shell for up to two days prior to serving, but the meringue is best made and eaten the same day.

▶ level: moderate   Makes one 9-inch pie, 6 to 8 slices

Lemon Curd
- 2 large eggs
- 5 large egg yolks
- 1½ cups plus 2 tablespoons sugar
- ¼ cup cornstarch
- Pinch of salt
- 1 cup fresh lemon juice
- ¼ cup water
- 1½ tablespoons grated lemon zest
- 4 tablespoons (½ stick) unsalted butter, at room temperature

Crust
- 1 prebaked 9-inch Traditional Pastry Piecrust dough for a single-crust pie shell (page 6)

Meringue
- 4 large egg whites, at room temperature
- ¼ teaspoon cream of tartar
- Pinch of salt
- ½ cup sugar
- 1 teaspoon pure vanilla extract

To prepare the lemon curd, whisk together the eggs, egg yolks, and sugar until the mixture is a pale yellow, about 2 minutes. Add the cornstarch and salt and continue whisking until all of the ingredients are well combined. Add the lemon juice, water, lemon zest, and butter. Continue whisking until fully incorporated.

Pour the mixture into a medium, heavy-bottomed saucepan and place it over medium heat. Whisk continuously, scraping the sides with a spatula and taking care not to burn the bottom. Keep the saucepan over heat until the mixture thickens and deepens in color, about 7 minutes. Remove the saucepan from the heat and continue to whisk the mixture for 1 more minute.

Pour the mixture into the prebaked piecrust. Cover the pie with plastic wrap and place it in the refrigerator to cool for at least 1 hour.

To prepare the meringue, using an electric mixer on high speed, beat the egg whites until they become foamy. Add the cream of tartar and salt and continue mixing until soft peaks form. Slowly add the sugar, 1 tablespoon at a time. Once all of the sugar has been added, add the vanilla and beat for 30 more seconds. The meringue should be light and fluffy. Test the meringue to see if it will hold by inserting your spatula into the meringue mixture and quickly pulling it out. If the meringue forms little peaks but does not fall, you have achieved the desired consistency. If the meringue does fall, continue beating and retesting with your spatula at 30-second intervals until the peaks remain in place when the spatula is removed.

Scrape the meringue out of the bowl and place it on top of the lemon curd in the pie shell. Smooth out the meringue to cover the entire pie and form a mound of meringue in the middle of the pie. Use a spatula to pat and lift the meringue across the top of the pie, forming peaks.

To brown the meringue, place the pie in an oven broiler on an oven rack placed in the middle position for 3 to 4 minutes (or until your desired brownness has been achieved); alternatively, use a kitchen torch (see page xviii). If you opt to use a kitchen torch, be careful to evenly spread the flame across the entire surface of the pie for a consistent finish.

Lemon Meringue Pie is best served cold and should be eaten the same day it's made.

Peach Crumb Pie

Peaches are at their best mid-July through September. When selecting peaches, look for those that do not have a green undertone—the sweetest peaches will come in warmer color shades and will omit a sweet odor. The most daunting part of this recipe is—surprise—actually peeling the peaches, but I have a great, simplified method for this process (see page 44). You can also make this pie with a Traditional Pastry double crust (page 5).

▶ level: easy   Makes one 9-inch pie, 6 to 8 slices

Crust and Topping

 1 recipe Traditional Pastry Piecrust dough for a 9-inch single-crust pie (page 5)
¼ cup heavy cream (to glaze the crimped pie edges)
   Cinnamon Sugar Crumb Topping (page 12)

Filling

 ½ cup sugar
 2 tablespoons cornstarch
 2 tablespoons quick-cooking tapioca (see page 46)
1½ teaspoons ground cinnamon
   Pinch of salt
 6 cups peeled ½-inch ripe but firm peach slices (approximately 8 large peaches)

Preheat the oven to 375°F.

To prepare the pie shell, on a clean, lightly floured work surface, roll out half a ball of dough with a rolling pin until it forms a 10-inch circle. Wrap the remaining half of the dough tightly in plastic wrap and reserve it in the refrigerator for future use for up to 5 days. Fold the circle in half, place it in a 9-inch pie plate so that the

edges of the circle drop over the rim, and unfold the dough to completely cover the pie plate. Using your thumb and index finger, crimp the edges of the pie shell. Brush the edges of the pie shell with heavy cream to create a perfect, golden brown finish. Set the pie shell to the side while you make the filling.

To prepare the filling, in a small bowl, mix together the sugar, cornstarch, tapioca, cinnamon, and salt. Place the peaches in a large bowl and sprinkle them with the sugar mixture, making sure all of the peaches are thoroughly coated. Place the peach mixture in the pie shell, distributing it evenly. Sprinkle the cinnamon sugar crumb topping over the peach filling, covering it completely.

To bake, place the pie plate on a baking sheet and bake for 50 to 60 minutes, or until the crust is golden brown and the juices are bubbling. Transfer the pie plate to a wire cooling rack and allow the pie to cool and set for 1½ hours before serving.

Peach Crumb Pie is best served at room temperature or warmed at 350°F for about 10 minutes. It will keep at room temperature overnight and can be stored in the refrigerator for up to 4 days.

How to Peel a Peach

. . . .

Fill a medium saucepan with enough water to fully immerse the peaches and bring it to a boil. Using a sharp knife, mark an X on the bottom of the peaches. Fill a medium bowl with ice-cold water and set it to the side. Once the saucepan has reached a boil, place the peaches in the boiling water for 30 seconds. Remove the peaches from the saucepan and immediately place them in your bowl of cold water. Once the peaches have cooled, start peeling off the skin at the X and then slice into wedges.

Peach-Blueberry Pie

I look forward to peach season like some people look forward to Christmas. Just think-ing about fresh, sliced peaches, seasoned perfectly and accompanied by a perfect crust, is enough to make my mouth water. The options for peach pie are virtually never ending. Not only is it equally tasty with a flaky traditional or sweet crumbly topping, but peaches also blend beautifully with other fruits, including blueberries, raspberries, dried cranberries, and strawberries. While we use blueberries here, try substituting a cup of your own favorite fruit (the fresher, the better). Be sure to also try this with Cin-namon Sugar Crumb Topping (page 12).

▶ level: easy   Makes one 9-inch pie, 6 to 8 slices

Crust

- 1   recipe Traditional Pastry Piecrust dough for a 9-inch double-crust pie (page 5)
- ½   cup heavy cream (to glaze the top crust and crimped pie edges)

Filling

- ¾   cup sugar
- 2   tablespoons cornstarch
- 2   tablespoons quick-cooking tapioca (see page 46)
- 1½   teaspoons ground cinnamon
-    Pinch of salt
- 3   cups peeled ½-inch ripe peach slices (approximately 4 large peaches)
- 1   cup fresh blueberries, washed, dried, and stemmed
- 1   tablespoon salted butter

Preheat the oven to 375°F.

To prepare the pie shell, divide the ball of dough in half, setting one half to the side. On a clean, lightly floured work surface, roll out the dough with a rolling pin

Baking with Tapioca

. . . .

Bakers frequently use tapioca as a thickening agent. When purchasing tapioca, be sure to select a quick-cooking (also labeled "instant") variety, rather than regular tapioca. Quick-cooking tapioca tolerates the baking process better than the regular variety, and provides the perfect pie filling consistency. Quick-cooking tapioca can be found in the baking aisle of your local grocery store, near the puddings.

until it forms a 10-inch circle. Fold the circle in half, place it in a 9-inch pie plate so that the edges of the circle drop over the rim, and unfold the dough to completely cover the pie plate. Set the pie shell to the side while you make the filling.

To prepare the filling, in a small bowl, mix together the sugar, cornstarch, tapioca, cinnamon, and salt. Place the peaches and blueberries in a large bowl and sprinkle them with the sugar mixture, making sure the fruit is thoroughly coated. Place the filling in the pie shell, distributing it evenly. Dot the filling with the butter.

To prepare the top crust, roll out the second half of the dough with a rolling pin until it forms a 10-inch circle. Fold the dough circle in half and place it over the filling, with the straight line of the half circle running down the middle of the pie. Unfold the circle so that the entire pie is covered. Using your thumb and index finger, crimp the edges of the pie together to seal in the filling, and then use a fork to puncture the top of the pie 5 or 6 times. Brush the top of the pie and crimped edges with heavy cream for a perfect, golden brown finish.

To bake, place the pie plate on a baking sheet and bake for 50 to 55 minutes, or until the crust is browned and the juices bubble over. Transfer the pie plate to a wire cooling rack and allow the pie to cool and set for 1½ hours before serving.

Peach-Blueberry Pie is best served either at room temperature or warmed at 350°F for about 10 minutes. It will keep at room temperature overnight and can be stored in the refrigerator for up to 4 days.

Pear Pie

Apple pie fans are drawn to this less tart, juicy alternative. You can also adjust the taste of the pie by choosing your favorite pear type. Yellow Bartlett pears are a great option because of their juicy sweetness. Red Bartlett or the more crisp and woodsy Bosc pear varieties also work well—or you can mix and match various pear types in a single pie to create your own blend of sweet, tangy, and aromatic flavors. You can also try this pie with Cinnamon Sugar Crumb Topping (page 12).

▶ level: easy   Makes one 9-inch pie, 6 to 8 slices

Crust
1 recipe Traditional Pastry Piecrust dough for a 9-inch double-crust pie (page 5)
½ cup heavy cream (to glaze the top crust and crimped pie edges)

Filling
¾ cup sugar
Pinch of ground cinnamon
1 tablespoon fresh lemon juice
2 teaspoons grated lemon zest
6 cups peeled ½-inch ripe pear slices (approximately 6 pears)
2½ tablespoons cornstarch
1 tablespoon salted butter

Preheat the oven to 425°F.

To prepare the pie shell, divide the ball of dough in half, setting one half to the side. On a clean, lightly floured work surface, roll out the dough with a rolling pin until it forms a 10-inch circle. Fold the circle in half, place it in a 9-inch pie plate so that the edges of the circle drop over the rim, and unfold the dough to completely cover the pie plate. Set the pie shell to the side while you make the filling.

To prepare the filling, in a small bowl, whisk together ½ cup of the sugar, the cinnamon, the lemon juice, and lemon zest. Place the pears in a large bowl and sprinkle them with the sugar mixture, making sure all of the pears are thoroughly coated. Set the pears aside for about 10 minutes, allowing them to soak up the flavor of the sugar mixture.

In a separate small bowl, whisk together the remaining ¼ cup sugar and the cornstarch. When the pears have set for 10 minutes, add the cornstarch mixture to the fruit, and toss the pears. Place the pear mixture in the pie shell, distributing it evenly. Dot the filling with the butter.

To prepare the top crust, roll out the second half of the dough with a rolling pin until it forms a 10-inch circle. Fold the dough circle in half and place it over the filling, with the straight line of the half circle running down the middle of the pie. Unfold the circle so that the entire pie is covered. Using your thumb and index finger, crimp the edges of the pie together to seal in the filling, and then use a fork to puncture the top of the pie 5 or 6 times. Brush the top of the pie and crimped edges with heavy cream to create a perfect, golden brown finish.

To bake, place the pie plate on a baking sheet and bake for 15 minutes. Reduce the temperature to 375°F and continue baking for approximately 45 minutes, or until the crust is golden brown and the juices are bubbling. Transfer the pie plate to a wire cooling rack and allow the pie to cool and set for 1½ hours before serving.

Pear Pie is best served either at room temperature or warmed at 350°F for about 10 minutes. It will keep at room temperature overnight and can be stored in the refrigerator for up to 4 days.

Pear-Raspberry Pie

Raspberries are one of those special fruits you can add to just about anything with great results. So, whenever I'm looking to spruce up more subtle tastes (like a pear filling), raspberries are my go-to fruit. Since pear and raspberry season overlap during the early fall months, Pear-Raspberry Pie is a nice alternative to the more traditional and expected harvesttime pies. You can also try this with Cinnamon Sugar Crumb Topping (page 12).

▶ level: easy   Makes one 9-inch pie, 6 to 8 slices

Crust
- 1 recipe Traditional Pastry Piecrust dough for a 9-inch double-crust pie (page 5)
- ½ cup heavy cream (to glaze the top crust and crimped pie edges)

Filling
- 3 cups peeled and seeded, ½-inch ripe Bartlett or Bosc pear slices (approximately 3 pears)
- ¾ cup fresh raspberries, washed and patted dry (be careful not to damage and break down the berries during the drying process)
- 1 cup sugar
- 1 tablespoon fresh lemon juice
- 1 teaspoon grated lemon zest
- 3 tablespoons cornstarch
- 1 tablespoon salted butter

Preheat the oven to 425°F.

To prepare the pie shell, divide the ball of dough in half, setting one half to the side. On a clean, lightly floured work surface, roll out the dough with a rolling pin until it forms a 10-inch circle. Fold the circle in half, place it in a 9-inch pie plate so that the edges of the circle drop over the rim, and unfold the dough to completely cover the pie plate. Set the pie shell to the side while you make the filling.

To prepare the filling, in a large bowl, mix together the pears, the raspberries, ¾ cup sugar, the lemon juice, and the lemon zest and let the ingredients sit for 5 minutes to bring out the juices. In a small bowl, whisk together the remaining ¼ cup sugar and the cornstarch. Sprinkle the sugar mixture over the fruit and toss until the fruit is thoroughly coated. Place the fruit mixture in the pie shell, distributing it evenly. Dot the filling with the butter.

To prepare the top crust, roll out the second half of the dough with a rolling pin until it forms a 10-inch circle. Fold the dough circle in half and place it over the filling, with the straight line of the half circle running down the middle of the pie. Unfold the circle so that the entire pie is covered. Using your thumb and index finger, crimp the edges of the pie together to seal in the filling, and then use a fork to puncture the top of the pie 5 or 6 times. Brush the top of the pie and crimped edges with heavy cream to create a perfect, golden brown finish.

To bake, place the pie plate on a baking sheet and bake for 15 minutes. Reduce the temperature to 375°F and continue baking for approximately 35 minutes, or until the pears are tender. Transfer the pie plate to a wire cooling rack and allow the pie to cool and set for 1½ hours before serving.

Pear-Raspberry Pie is best served either at room temperature or warmed at 350°F for about 10 minutes. It will keep at room temperature overnight and can be stored in the refrigerator for up to 4 days.

Pear-Apple-Cranberry Crumb Pie

Talk about zing! This pie will turn even the most bland and basic of winter dinners into a completely memorable meal. The red color of fresh cranberries mixed in with the pale hues of apples and pears makes for a gorgeous presentation. But that's just the beginning. This pie also beautifully combines the tartness of cranberries with the sweetness of apples and pears. To really highlight the spectacular color of this pie, use either the Cinnamon Sugar Crumb Topping or the Walnut Crumb Topping (page 14). Or if you want to highlight the tartness of the cranberries, I recommend using the double-crust Traditional Pastry Piecrust (page 5).

▶ level: moderate   Makes one 9-inch pie, 6 to 8 slices

Crust and topping

1 recipe Traditional Pastry Piecrust dough for a 9-inch single-crust pie (page 5)

¼ cup heavy cream (to glaze the crimped pie edges)

Cinnamon Sugar Crumb Topping (page 12)

Filling

¾ cup sugar

2 tablespoons unbleached all-purpose flour

1 tablespoon ground cinnamon

Dash of ground nutmeg

4 medium pears, peeled, cored, and cut into ½-inch pieces

4 medium Cortland apples, peeled, cored, and cut into ½-inch chunks

½ cup fresh or thawed frozen cranberries, coarsely chopped

Preheat the oven to 425°F.

To prepare the pie shell, on a clean, lightly floured work surface, roll out half a ball of dough with a rolling pin until it forms a 10-inch circle. Wrap the remaining half of the dough tightly in plastic wrap, and reserve it in the refrigerator for future use for up to 5 days. Fold the circle in half, place it in a 9-inch pie plate so that the edges of the circle drop over the rim, and unfold the dough to completely cover the pie plate. Using your thumb and index finger, crimp the edges of the pie shell. Brush the edges of the pie shell with heavy cream to create a perfect, golden brown finish. Set the pie shell to the side while you make the filling.

To prepare the filling, in a large bowl, mix together the sugar, flour, cinnamon, and nutmeg. Add the pears, apples, and chopped cranberries, tossing until they are thoroughly coated with the sugar mixture. Place the fruit mixture in the pie shell, distributing it evenly. Sprinkle the Cinnamon Sugar Crumb Topping over the apple-cranberry filling, covering it completely.

To bake, place the pie plate on a baking sheet and bake for 15 minutes. Reduce the temperature to 375°F and continue baking for approximately 45 minutes, or until the crust is golden brown and the juices are bubbling. Transfer the pie plate to a wire cooling rack and allow the pie to cool and set for 1½ hours before serving.

Pear-Apple-Cranberry Crumb Pie is best served either at room temperture or warmed at 350°F for about 10 minutes. It will keep at room temperature overnight and can be stored in the refrigerator for up to 4 days.

Fresh Cranberries Versus Dried Cranberries

. . . .

The fresh or frozen cranberries used in the pear-apple-cranberry-crumb pie provide a tart, tangy, crisp note to contrast the sweeter flavors of apple and pear. Dried cranberries (such as those used in the Apple-Cranberry Crumb Pie, page 000), on the other hand, are on the sweeter side because most manufacturers add sugar.

Pear-Cranberry Pie with Walnut Crumb

Although it's not the most traditional holiday dessert, this pie pairs well with a Christmas roast. The cranberries add a festive note, while the walnut crumb adds an extra bit of crunchy texture. This pie looks just as delicious as it tastes.

▶ level: moderate   Makes one 9-inch pie, 6 to 8 slices

Crust and Topping

1 recipe Traditional Pastry Piecrust dough for a 9-inch single-crust pie (page 5)

Walnut Crumb Topping (page 14)

Filling

1½ cups fresh cranberries

½ cup plus 1 tablespoon sugar

4 medium, ripe Bartlett or Bosc pears, peeled, cored, and cut into ½-inch cubes

1 tablespoon fresh lemon juice

1 tablespoon grated orange zest

1½ tablespoons cornstarch

¼ teaspoon ground cinnamon

Dash of ground nutmeg

Preheat oven to 425°F.

To prepare the pie shell, on a clean, lightly floured work surface, roll out half a ball of dough with a rolling pin until it forms a 10-inch circle. Wrap the remaining half of the dough tightly in plastic wrap and reserve it in the refrigerator for future use for up to 5 days. Fold the circle in half, place it in a 9-inch pie plate so that the edges of the circle drop over the rim, and unfold the dough to completely cover the pie plate. Using your thumb and index finger, crimp the edges of the pie shell.

Brush the edges of the pie shell with heavy cream to create a perfect, golden brown finish. Set the pie shell to the side while you make the filling.

To prepare the filling, place the cranberries and ½ cup sugar in a food processor and pulse 6 to 8 times, or until the cranberries are coarsely chopped. Transfer the cranberry mixture to a large bowl, and add the pears, lemon juice, and orange zest. Let the fruit sit for about 10 minutes so that the juices can seep through. In a separate small bowl, combine the remaining 1 tablespoon sugar, the cornstarch, cinnamon, and nutmeg. Add the sugar mixture to the fruit and combine thoroughly. Place the fruit mixture in the pie shell, distributing it evenly. Sprinkle the walnut crumb topping over the filling, covering it completely.

To bake, place the pie plate on a baking sheet and bake for 15 minutes. Reduce the temperature to 375°F and continue baking for 40 to 45 minutes, or until the pears are tender and the juices are bubbling. Transfer the pie plate to a wire cooling rack and allow the pie to cool and set for 1½ hours before serving.

Pear-Cranberry Pie with walnut crumb is best served either at room temperature or warmed at 350°F for about 10 minutes. It will keep at room temperature overnight and can be stored in the refrigerator for up to 4 days.

Pineapple Crumb Pie

When Kelly told me he was going to try making a pineapple pie, I thought he was crazy. I've heard of pineapple in a lot of things . . . but pie? Wanting no part in this, I told him to go for it, and walked away. A few days later, I found myself biting into Kelly's first attempt. It wasn't bad—granted, it wasn't great either—but I began to think he was on to something. With my curiosity piqued, I decided to take a stab at it myself. Today, Pineapple Crumb Pie is one of the more popular pies we sell. For a more tropical variation of this pie, you can also try it with Macadamia-Coconut Crumb Topping (page 13).

▶ level: easy   Makes one 9-inch pie, 6 to 8 slices

Crust and Topping
1   recipe Traditional Pastry Piecrust dough for a 9-inch single-crust pie (page 5)
¼   cup heavy cream (to glaze the crimped pie edges)
    Cinnamon Sugar Crumb Topping (page 12)

Filling
½   cup sugar (to taste, depending on the sweetness of the fruit)
1   teaspoon ground cinnamon
1   medium, ripe pineapple, peeled, cored, and cut into ½-inch cubes (4 cups)
1   tablespoon salted butter

Preheat the oven to 425°F.

To prepare the pie shell, divide the ball of dough in half, setting one half to the side. On a clean, lightly floured work surface, roll out the dough with a rolling pin until it forms a 10-inch circle. Wrap the remaining half of the dough tightly in plastic wrap and reserve it in the refrigerator for future use for up to 5 days. Fold the circle in half, place it in a 9-inch pie plate so that the edges of the circle drop over the rim, and unfold the dough to completely cover the pie plate. Using your thumb and index finger, crimp the edges of the pie shell. Brush the edges of the pie shell with heavy cream to create a perfect, golden brown finish. Set the pie shell to the side while you make the filling.

To prepare the filling, in a small bowl, whisk together the sugar and cinnamon. Place the pineapple in a large bowl and toss it with the sugar mixture, making sure that all of the pineapple is thoroughly coated. Place the pineapple mixture in the pie shell, distributing it evenly. Dot the filling with the butter. Sprinkle the cinnamon sugar crumb topping over the pineapple filling, covering it completely.

To bake, place the pie plate on a baking sheet and bake for 15 minutes. Reduce the heat to 375°F and continue baking for 40 minutes, or until the juices bubble over and the crumb mixture has browned. Transfer the pie plate to a wire cooling rack and allow the pie to cool and set for 1½ hours before serving.

Pineapple Crumb Pie is best served either at room temperature or warmed at 350°F for about 10 minutes. It will keep at room temperature overnight and can be stored in the refrigerator for up to 4 days.

Pineapple Time-saver

Many grocery stores now offer precut and cored pineapples. If you're short on time, this option is a great way to make this already simple pie even easier.

Pineapple-Mango Pie
with Macadamia-Coconut Crumb

When I first entered this pie in the 2010 National Pie Championships, I called it Tropical Explosion, and that pretty much tells you everything you need to know about the taste. Pineapples don't ripen after they're picked, so be sure to look for pineapples that are green only at the crown with a golden yellow body (green bodies indicate they aren't ripe). Smell a pineapple at its stem to make sure it has a sweet odor. Even in the dark, cold days of winter, the fresh, tangy flavors of pineapple and mango floating under a coconut-infused topping will conjure up images of a hot Caribbean beach.

▶ level: moderate   Makes one 9-inch pie, 6 to 8 slices

Crust and Topping
- 1 recipe Traditional Pastry Piecrust dough for a 9-inch single-crust pie (page 5)
- ¼ cup heavy cream (to glaze the crimped pie edges)
  Macadamia-Coconut Crumb Topping (page 13)

Filling
- ½ cup sugar (to taste, depending on the sweetness of the fruit)
- 1 teaspoon ground cinnamon
- 2 cups ½-inch cubed ripe mango
- 2 cups ½-inch cubed ripe pineapple
- 1 tablespoon salted butter

Preheat the oven to 425°F.

To prepare the pie shell, on a clean, lightly floured work surface, roll out half a ball of dough with a rolling pin until it forms a 10-inch circle. Wrap the remaining half of the dough tightly in plastic wrap and reserve it in the refrigerator for future use for up to 5 days. Fold the circle in half, place it in a 9-inch pie plate so that the

edges of the circle drop over the rim, and unfold the dough to completely cover the pie plate. Using your thumb and index finger, crimp the edges of the pie shell. Brush the edges of the pie shell with heavy cream to create a perfect, golden brown finish. Set the pie shell to the side while you make the filling.

To prepare the filling, in a small bowl, whisk together the sugar and cinnamon. Place the mangoes and pineapple in a large bowl and toss them with the sugar mixture, making sure that all of the fruit is thoroughly coated. Place the pineapple-mango mixture in the pie shell, distributing it evenly. Dot the filling with the butter. Sprinkle the macadamia-coconut crumb topping over the filling, covering it completely.

To bake, place the pie plate on a baking sheet and bake for 15 minutes. Reduce the heat to 350°F and continue baking for approximately 45 minutes, or until the crust achieves a nice shade of golden brown. Transfer the pie plate to a wire cooling rack and allow the pie to cool and set for 1½ hours before serving.

Pineapple-Mango Pie with Macadamia-Coconut Crumb is best served either at room temperature or warmed at 350°F for about 10 minutes. It will keep at room temperature overnight and can be stored in the refrigerator for up to 4 days.

Choosing the Right Pie Plate for Pineapple Pies

Pineapple pies should not be baked in a glass or ceramic pie plate due to their excess juices, which will impede the baking process. The bottom crust of pineapple pies will bake best when cooked in a disposable or metal pie plate, which allows the crust to brown properly.

Pumpkin Pie

One of the things Michele's Pies is best known for is our Pumpkin Pie. The secret to our success is simple: Use fresh pumpkins, never canned. I recommend using the sugar pumpkin variety for this recipe because not only do these pumpkins have the most flavor, but their dark orange flesh will make your pie a beautiful, deep, rich orange color.

Processing pumpkins does take some extra effort, but it's worth it when you see everyone's faces light up as they taste their first bites of this special pie after Thanksgiving dinner. To be honest, when I first opened up the shop, I had to convince my own staff to take the additional step of pumpkin processing in the midst of the Thanksgiving rush. After hearing a few of them make the argument for using a premade canned pumpkin filling, I decided to prove my point. I sat the entire staff down for a blind taste test, during which I served them pumpkin pies made from a variety of canned pumpkin fillings and a pie made from my own freshly processed pumpkins. Unanimously, they chose the freshly processed pumpkin pie as the best of the bunch. Since then, I've never heard a single complaint about the extra effort. (For processing instructions, see page 65).

▶ level: challenging   Makes one 9-inch pie, 6 to 8 slices

Crust

1 recipe Traditional Pastry Piecrust dough for a 9-inch single-crust pie (page 5)

¼ cup heavy cream (to glaze the crimped pie edges)

Filling

2 cups fresh processed pumpkin (a 5-pound sugar pumpkin yields about 2 cups; see Note at end of recipe)

One 14-ounce can sweetened condensed milk

2 large eggs

1½   teaspoons ground cinnamon

½   teaspoon salt

Preheat the oven to 425°F.

To prepare the pie shell, on a clean, lightly floured work surface, roll out half a ball of dough with a rolling pin until it forms a 10-inch circle. Wrap the remaining half of the dough tightly in plastic wrap and reserve it in the refrigerator for future use for up to 5 days. Fold the circle in half, place it in a 9-inch pie plate so that the edges of the circle drop over the rim, and unfold the dough to completely cover the pie plate. Using your thumb and index finger, crimp the edges of the pie shell. Brush the edges of the pie shell with heavy cream to create a perfect, golden brown finish. Set the pie shell to the side while you make the filling.

To prepare the filling, in a large bowl, combine the pumpkin, condensed milk, eggs, cinnamon, and salt. Make sure to scrape the sides of the bowl several times to fully incorporate all ingredients. Pour the pumpkin filling into the pie shell, distributing it evenly.

To bake, place the pie plate on a baking sheet and bake for 10 minutes. Reduce the heat to 375°F and continue baking for approximately 35 minutes, or until the pie is firm in the middle. Transfer the pie plate to a wire cooling rack and allow the pie to cool and set for 1½ hours before serving.

Pumpkin Pie is best served cold or at room temperature. It can be stored in the refrigerator for up to 4 days.

Note: Alternatively, use a 15-ounce can of pumpkin filling, but I strongly encourage you to try the fresh pumpkin variety.

Maple Pumpkin Pie with Pecan Streusel

This pie will always have a special meaning to me because it was the centerpiece of the bake-off of my dreams! I remember watching Food Network programs as a teenager, thinking, "I would love to be on these shows!" Well, thanks to Bobby Flay, I got the chance to prove that my pies could compete with the best. In November 2009 he challenged me to a pumpkin pie throwdown on *Throwdown! with Bobby Flay*. Although Bobby ultimately won the throwdown, he told me my version was "one of the best pumpkin pies I have ever eaten." I like to serve this pie with a dollop of Maple Whipped Cream (page 194).

▶ level: challenging   Makes one 9-inch pie, 6 to 8 slices

Crust
- 1 recipe Traditional Pastry Piecrust dough for a 9-inch single-crust pie (page 5)
- ¼ cup heavy cream (to glaze the crimped pie edges)

Pecan Streusel
- ¾ cup pecans, toasted and chopped
- ¼ cup firmly packed light brown sugar
- 2 tablespoons unbleached all-purpose flour
- 2 teaspoons ground cinnamon
- 2 tablespoons unsalted butter

Pumpkin Filling
- 2 cups fresh processed pumpkin (see Note at end of recipe)
- 2 tablespoons unbleached all-purpose flour
- ⅓ cup firmly packed dark brown sugar
- ½ teaspoon ground nutmeg
- ½ teaspoon ground cinnamon

½   teaspoon salt

1⅓   cups heavy cream

1   cup Grade B Vermont maple syrup

3   large eggs

Preheat the oven to 425°F.

To prepare the pie shell, on a clean, lightly floured work surface, roll out half a ball of dough with a rolling pin until it forms a 10-inch circle. Wrap the remaining half of the dough tightly in plastic wrap and reserve it in the refrigerator for future use for up to 5 days. Fold the circle in half, place it in a 9-inch pie plate so that the edges of the circle drop over the rim, and unfold the dough to completely cover the pie plate. Using your thumb and index finger, crimp the edges of the pie shell. Brush the edges of the pie shell with heavy cream to create a perfect, golden brown finish. Set the pie shell to the side while you make the streusel and filling.

To prepare the streusel, in a medium bowl, mix together the pecans, brown sugar, flour, and cinnamon. Toss together, making sure the pecans are thoroughly coated. Cube the butter and add it to the mixture. Using a pastry blender or your fingertips, crumble the mixture to form pea-size streusel. Chill the streusel in the refrigerator until the pie is mostly baked.

To prepare the filling, using an electric mixer on medium speed, mix together the pumpkin, flour, brown sugar, nutmeg, cinnamon, and salt until smooth. Scrape the sides of the bowl well and mix again. When the mixture is thoroughly combined, add the heavy cream and maple syrup, scraping the bowl several times while mixing. In a separate small bowl, beat the eggs and then mix them into the pumpkin mixture. Pour the pumpkin filling into the pie shell, distributing it evenly.

To bake, place the pie plate on a baking sheet and bake for 15 minutes. Reduce the heat to 350°F and continue baking for 30 minutes, or until the filling is almost firm in the middle. Remove the pie from the oven and sprinkle the pecan streusel over the top, covering the pie completely. Place the pie back in the oven for approximately 10 more minutes, or until the pie is firm in the middle and the pecan streusel is golden. Total baking time should be 50 to 55 minutes. Transfer the pie plate to a wire cooling rack and allow the pie to cool and set for 1½ hours before serving. If you choose, add a dollop of Maple Whipped Cream (page 194) to each slice to serve.

Maple Pumpkin Pie is best served cold or at room temperature. It can be stored in the refrigerator for up to 4 days.

Note: For pumpkin processing instructions, see page 65; if fresh pumpkin is unavailable, use 2 cups canned Libby's 100% Pure Pumpkin.

What Are Sugar Pumpkins?

· · · · · · · · · · · ·

Sugar pumpkins are a variety of pumpkin different from those you carve for Halloween (field pumpkins). Sometimes referred to as pie pumpkins, sugar pumpkins are small, tender, and sweet, with a dark orange flesh. The inside of a sugar pumpkin is less hollow and stringy than the inside of a field pumpkin, giving you lots of flesh to use for pumpkin pie.

How to Process Fresh Pumpkins

Here's what you'll need:

One 5-pound sugar pumpkin   Steamer

Sharp knife   Cheesecloth

Spoon   Food processor

Begin by cutting the sugar pumpkin in half with a sharp knife. Use a spoon to scoop out the seeds and clear the stringy matter out of the pumpkin's interior.

Place the pumpkin halves in a steamer and steam for 20 minutes or until they become soft enough for a knife to be easily inserted through the flesh. Remove the pumpkin halves from the steamer and allow them to cool for a few minutes.

Once the pumpkin has cooled, peel off the skin with a knife and place the pumpkin flesh between a piece of cheesecloth, then fold the cheesecloth in half. Press down on the pumpkin until the majority of the water has been drained through the cheesecloth. Be diligent: Pumpkins retain a lot of water, so you'll have to squeeze the pumpkin several times.

Place the pumpkin flesh in a food processor and puree until it achieves a smooth consistency, with no chunks. Pour the pumpkin puree into a bowl and *voilà*! You have an amazing pumpkin puree in a rich shade of orange. Pumpkin puree keeps for up to 8 months frozen.

Pumpkin Chiffon Pie

This pie packs in all of the traditional pumpkin holiday flavor, but with a much lighter and airier texture than traditional pumpkin pie, making this a great alternative at the end of a heavy, multicourse meal. Serve with a dollop of Whipped Cream (page 193).

▶ level: challenging   Makes one 9-inch pie, 6 to 8 slices

Crust
1 prebaked 9-inch Traditional Pastry Piecrust dough for a single-crust pie shell (page 6)

Filling
1 envelope unflavored gelatin

¾ cup ice-cold water

1 cup fresh processed (see processing instructions, page 65) or canned pumpkin

4 large egg yolks

1 cup sugar

1 cup whole milk

½ teaspoon salt

¼ teaspoon ground nutmeg

1½ teaspoons ground cinnamon

2 tablespoons salted butter

4 large egg whites

To prepare the filling, pour the gelatin into a small bowl with the cold water and allow it to soften (approximately 5 minutes). While the gelatin is softening, place the pumpkin, egg yolks, ½ cup sugar, milk, salt, nutmeg, cinnamon, and butter in the top of a double boiler over medium heat. Stir continuously for approximately 10 minutes, or until a custard consistency is achieved. Once you have a custardlike texture, add the softened gelatin, again mixing well. Remove the filling from the heat, pour it into a bowl, and put it in the refrigerator to chill for at least 1 hour.

Once the pumpkin filling has cooled, in a separate bowl, beat the egg whites and the remaining ½ cup sugar until the mixture is stiff and meringuelike. Fold the egg whites into the cooled pumpkin filling. Pour the filling into the prebaked crust and refrigerate for at least 5 hours before serving. If you choose, add a dollop of Whipped Cream (page 193) to each slice to serve.

Pumpkin Chiffon Pie is best served cold or at room temperature. It can be stored in the refrigerator for up to 4 days.

Raspberry Crumb Pie

Taste testing is one of the great perks of my job. Every summer when our first batch of Raspberry Crumb Pies comes out of the oven, I take one home with me so that my family and I can perform "quality assurance." It's a tough job, but somebody has to do it! Raspberries are at their best in the midsummer months. For best results, seek out raspberries that are slightly soft and plump. Raspberries continue to ripen after they are picked and have a short shelf-life, so try to make this pie within a day or two of bringing home your raspberries. Raspberry pie is equally good made with a traditional pastry piecrust (as photographed here with a lattice topping) or a Cinnamon Sugar Crumb Topping, but, I have to say, I'm partial to the crumb topping—the sweetness is a lovely complement to the raspberries' tartness. Serve with a scoop of vanilla ice cream or a dollop of Whipped Cream (page 193). This pie can also be made with the Traditional Pastry double crust (page 5).

▶ level: easy   Makes one 9-inch pie, 6 to 8 slices

Crust and topping
- 1 recipe Traditional Pastry Piecrust dough for a 9-inch single-crust pie (page 5)
- ¼ cup heavy cream (to glaze the crimped pie edges)
  Cinnamon Sugar Crumb Topping (page 12)

Filling
- 4 cups fresh raspberries
- ¾ cup sugar
- ½ cup unbleached all-purpose flour
- ½ teaspoon ground cinnamon

Preheat the oven to 425°F.

To prepare the pie shell, on a clean, lightly floured work surface, roll out half a ball of dough with a rolling pin until it forms a 10-inch circle. Wrap the remaining half of the dough tightly in plastic wrap and reserve it in the refrigerator for future use for up to 5 days. Fold the circle in half, place it in a 9-inch pie plate so that the edges of the circle drop over the rim, and unfold the dough to completely cover the pie plate. Using your thumb and index finger, crimp the edges of the pie shell. Brush the edges of the pie shell with heavy cream to create a perfect, golden brown finish. Set the pie shell to the side while you make the filling.

To prepare the filling, gently and thoroughly wash and dry the raspberries, then set them aside in a medium bowl. In a small bowl, combine the sugar, flour, and cinnamon. Sprinkle the sugar mixture over the raspberries, tossing them gently until they are thoroughly coated. Gently place the raspberries in the pie shell, taking care not to break down the berries. Sprinkle the Cinnamon Sugar Crumb topping over the raspberry filling, covering it completely.

To bake, place the pie plate on a baking sheet and bake for 15 minutes. Reduce the heat to 375°F and continue baking for 40 minutes. Transfer the pie plate to a wire cooling rack and allow the pie to cool and set for 1½ hours before serving. If you choose, add a dollop of whipped cream to each slice to serve.

Raspberry Crumb Pie is best served either at room temperature or warmed at 350°F for about 10 minutes. It will keep at room temperature overnight and can be stored in the refrigerator for up to 4 days.

Rhubarb Pie

This pie is one of those treats you have to enjoy while the weather is warm because rhubarb is in season only from April to September. When selecting rhubarb, look for firm, glossy stalks. Be sure to cut off all of the leaves of a rhubarb stalk—they are toxic to humans. Wash the rhubarb stalk well and then peel the stringy skin to get to the core of this celerylike vegetable. Try this pie with the Cinnamon Sugar Crumb Topping (page 12) for a nice contrast to rhubarb's naturally tart taste.

▶ level: easy   Makes one 9-inch pie, 6 to 8 slices

Crust

- 1 recipe Traditional Pastry Piecrust dough for a 9-inch double-crust pie (page 5)
- ½ cup heavy cream (to glaze the top crust and crimped pie edges)

Filling

- 1½ cups sugar
- 2 tablespoons cornstarch
- 2 tablespoons quick-cooking tapioca (see page 46)
- Pinch of salt
- 6 cups trimmed ½-inch-thick rhubarb slices (approximately 8 large rhubarb stalks)
- 1 tablespoon unsalted butter

Preheat the oven to 375°F.

To prepare the pie shell, on a clean, lightly floured work surface, roll out half a ball of dough with a rolling pin until it forms a 10-inch circle. Fold the circle in half, place it in a 9-inch pie plate so that the edges of the circle drop over the rim, and unfold the dough to completely cover the pie plate. Set the pie shell to the side while you make the filling.

To prepare the filling, in a small bowl, mix together the sugar, cornstarch, tapioca, and salt. Place the rhubarb in a large bowl and sprinkle it with the sugar mixture, making sure the rhubarb is thoroughly coated. Place the rhubarb in the pie shell, distributing it evenly. Dot the filling with the butter.

To prepare the top crust, roll out the second half of the dough with a rolling pin until it forms a 10-inch circle. Fold the dough circle in half and place it over the filling, with the straight line of the half circle running down the middle of the pie. Unfold the circle so that the entire pie is covered. Using your thumb and index finger, crimp the edges of the pie together to seal in the filling, and then use a fork to puncture the top of the pie 5 or 6 times. Brush the top of the pie and crimped edges with heavy cream to create a perfect, golden brown finish.

To bake, place the pie plate on a baking sheet and bake for 50 to 60 minutes, or until the crust is golden brown. Transfer the pie plate to a wire cooling rack and allow the pie to cool and set for 1½ hours before serving.

Rhubarb Pie is best served at room temperature or warmed to 350°F for about 10 minutes. It will keep at room temperature overnight and can be stored in the refrigerator for up to 4 days.

Strawberry-Rhubarb Crumb Pie

This pie is a study in contrasts, with strawberries acting as the perfect natural sweetener for rhubarb's tartness. Enjoy this pie between June and July, when strawberries are at their prime, coinciding with the rhubarb season. As with Rhubarb Pie (page 71), if you prefer a less sweet pie, try this recipe using the traditional pastry double crust.

▶ level: moderate   Makes one 9-inch pie, 6 to 8 slices

Crust and Topping

- 1 recipe Traditional Pastry Piecrust dough for a 9-inch single-crust pie (page 5)
- ¼ cup heavy cream (to glaze the crimped pie edges)
  Cinnamon Sugar Crumb Topping (page 12)

Filling

- 1 cup sugar
- 2 tablespoons cornstarch
- 2 tablespoons quick-cooking tapioca (see page 46)
  Pinch of salt
- 3 cups hulled and quartered (lengthwise) strawberries (approximately 1 pound strawberries)
- 3 cups trimmed ½-inch-thick slices rhubarb (approximately 4 large rhubarb stalks)
- 1 tablespoon unsalted butter, cold and cut into small pieces

Preheat the oven to 375°F.

   To prepare the pie shell, on a clean, lightly floured work surface, roll out half a ball of dough with a rolling pin until it forms a 10-inch circle. Wrap the remaining half of dough tightly in plastic wrap and reserve it in the refrigerator for future use for up to 5 days. Fold the circle in half, place it in a 9-inch pie plate so that the edges of the circle drop over the rim, and unfold the dough to completely cover the pie plate. Brush the edges of the pie shell with heavy cream to create a perfect, golden brown finish. Set the pie shell to the side while you make the filling.

To prepare the filling, in a small bowl, mix together the sugar, cornstarch, tapioca, and salt. Place the strawberries and rhubarb in a large bowl, and sprinkle with the sugar mixture, making sure all of the fruit is thoroughly coated. Immediately transfer the strawberry-rhubarb filling to the pie shell (if left sitting too long, these fruits will create a lot of juice, resulting in a soggy pie) and dot the filling with the butter. Sprinkle the cinnamon sugar crumb topping over the strawberry-rhubarb filling, covering it completely.

To bake, place the pie plate on a baking sheet and bake for 50 to 60 minutes, or until the crust is golden brown and the filling is thick and bubbling. Transfer the pie plate to a wire cooling rack and allow the pie to cool and set for 1½ hours before serving.

Strawberry-Rhubarb Crumb Pie is best served at room temperature or warmed to 350°F for about 10 minutes. It will keep at room temperature overnight and can be stored in the refrigerator for up to 4 days.

Sweet Potato Pie

Think of this pie as Pumpkin Pie's cousin. The creamy potato puree (best when made from locally grown sweet potatoes) makes for a dense, sweet pie. Like pumpkin pie, this southern staple has a deep, rich orange color that, topped with a dollop of Whipped Cream (page 193) or cinnamon ice cream, makes for a beautiful centerpiece to your holiday dessert table.

▶ level: challenging   Makes one 9-inch pie, 6 to 8 slices

Crust

- 1 recipe Traditional Pastry Piecrust dough for a 9-inch single-crust pie (page 5)
- ¼ cup heavy cream (to glaze the crimped pie edges)

Filling

- 2 large sweet potatoes (approximately 1 pound)
- ⅓ cup granulated sugar
- ⅓ cup firmly packed dark brown sugar
- 3 large eggs
- 1 large egg yolk
- 1 cup half-and-half
- 1 teaspoon pure vanilla extract
- 1 teaspoon ground cinnamon
- ½ teaspoon ground nutmeg
- Pinch of salt

Preheat the oven to 400°F.

To prepare the pie shell, on a clean, lightly floured work surface, roll out half a ball of dough with a rolling pin until it forms a 10-inch circle. Wrap the remaining half of the dough tightly in plastic wrap and reserve it in the refrigerator for future

use for up to 5 days. Fold the circle in half, place it in a 9-inch pie plate so that the edges of the circle drop over the rim, and unfold the dough to completely cover the pie plate. Using your thumb and index finger, crimp the edges of the pie shell. Brush the edges of the pie shell with heavy cream to create a perfect, golden brown finish. Set the pie shell to the side while you make the filling.

To prepare the filling, slice the sweet potatoes with a paring knife several times to score them. Place the sweet potatoes on a baking sheet and bake for approximately 50 minutes, or until they are tender. You can check to see if the potatoes are done with either your paring knife or a fork—if the utensil is easy to insert and comes out clean, the potatoes are cooked. Set the potatoes aside to cool. Once they are thoroughly cooled, peel them carefully, removing all of the skin.

Place the peeled potatoes in a food processor and process them until they are a smooth puree, with no lumps. Depending on the size of the potatoes, you may have some extra puree. If so, this is a great side dish for any dinner.

Place the puree in a medium bowl. Add the granulated sugar, brown sugar, eggs, and egg yolk and mix until they are well combined. Add the half-and-half, vanilla, cinnamon, nutmeg, and salt. Pour the sweet potato mixture into the pie shell, distributing it evenly.

To bake, place the pie plate on a baking sheet and bake for 15 minutes. Reduce the temperature to 350°F and continue baking for approximately 30 minutes, or until the pie is as firm in the middle as elsewhere. Transfer the pie plate to a wire cooling rack and allow the pie to cool and set for 1½ hours before serving. If you choose, add a dollop of whipped cream to each slice to serve.

Sweet Potato Pie is best served cold or at room temperature. It can be stored in the refrigerator for up to 4 days.

3

nut pies

· ·

Although apple pie is most often cited as the quintessential American dessert, there's a good argument that this title should actually be bestowed upon Pecan Pie, particularly in the South, where the majority of pecans are grown.

The nut pies in this chapter primarily center around pecans because their rich, buttery flavor lends itself so well to pies and other desserts, but you'll also find a few walnut-based recipes here as well. One of the greatest things about nut pies is that they are generally quite easy to make. It's all about adding a few ingredients for extra flavoring to create the rich, sweet or savory pie of your choosing. Speaking of choices, you can also mix and match with these recipes, substituting your favorite nut.

Our shop's signature pie, Chocolate-Pecan-Bourbon Pie (page 83), is also found in this chapter. When it was featured on *Good Morning America*'s "Best Slice Challenge," I actually had a customer drive more than seven hundred miles from Ohio to Connecticut just to sample one of these pies for herself. Although I was flattered that someone would go to such lengths to try one of my creations, I've included the recipe here so that anyone can now make this award-winning pie in his or her own kitchen.

Pecan Pie

One of the greatest compliments I've received in my professional life thus far was being told that I "make pecan pie like a true Southerner." In this chapter, you'll find a few variations, but nice as it is to mix things up sometimes, there's also much to be said for the clean taste and sweet flavor of traditional Pecan Pie. In addition to capping off holiday meals, it is also a great way to end a summer barbecue.

▶ level: easy   Makes one 9-inch pie, 6 to 8 slices

Crust

- 1 recipe Traditional Pastry Piecrust dough for a 9-inch single crust pie (page 5)
- ¼ cup heavy cream (to glaze the crimped pie edges)

Filling

- 1¼ cups dark corn syrup
- 3 extra-large eggs, lightly beaten
- ¾ cup sugar
- 2 tablespoons salted butter, melted
- 1½ teaspoons pure vanilla extract
- 2 cups pecan halves

Preheat the oven to 350°F.

To prepare the pie shell, on a clean, lightly floured work surface, roll out half a ball of dough with a rolling pin until it forms a 10-inch circle. Wrap the remaining half of the dough tightly in plastic wrap and reserve it in the refrigerator for future use for up to 5 days. Fold the circle in half, place it in a 9-inch pie plate so that the edges of the circle drop over the rim, and unfold the dough to completely cover the pie plate. Using your thumb and index finger, crimp the edges of the pie shell.

Brush the edges of the pie shell with heavy cream to create a perfect, golden brown finish. Set the pie shell to the side while you make the filling.

To prepare the filling, using an electric mixer on medium speed, mix together the corn syrup, eggs, sugar, butter, and vanilla until a light brown color is achieved, about 3 minutes. Stir in the pecans with a spoon or spatula, making sure they are incorporated throughout. Place the filling in the pie shell, distributing it evenly.

To bake, place the pie plate on a baking sheet and bake for 55 to 60 minutes, or until the pie is firm in the middle. Transfer the pie plate to a wire cooling rack and allow the pie to cool and set for 1 hour before serving.

Pecan Pie is best served at room temperature. It can be stored in the refrigerator for up to 5 days.

Butterscotch Pecan Pie Variation

Prepare the pecan pie filling according to the recipe above. To assemble the pie, sprinkle ½ cup butterscotch chips across the bottom of the pie shell, distributing them evenly. Add the pecan filling on top of the butterscotch chips. Bake as directed.

AWARD
NATIONAL PIE
CHAMPIONSHIPS
WINNER

Chocolate-Pecan-Bourbon Pie

This is not only our signature pie but, more than that, I consider it my "lucky" pie. In addition to its being our first National Pie Championships winner, our customers voted it into *Good Morning America*'s "Best Slice Challenge" contest. The segment aired just a few days before my first Thanksgiving in the shop, making it nearly impossible to keep this pie stocked for the holidays. To really blow your guests away, I recommend serving this pie warm with a drizzle of Bourbon Sauce (page 190) or a scoop of vanilla ice cream on top.

▶ level: moderate   Makes one 9-inch pie, 6 to 8 slices

Crust

1	recipe Traditional Pastry Piecrust dough for a 9-inch single-crust pie (page 5)
¼	cup heavy cream (to glaze the crimped pie edges)

Filling

3	large eggs, at room temperature
½	cup plus 1 tablespoon sugar
1¼	cups dark corn syrup
½	tablespoon pure vanilla extract
1	tablespoon bourbon
5	tablespoons unsalted butter, melted and kept warm
1½	cups chopped pecans
¾	cup semisweet chocolate chips

Preheat the oven to 350°F.

To prepare the pie shell, on a clean, lightly floured work surface, roll out half a ball of dough with a rolling pin until it forms a 10-inch circle. Wrap the remaining half of the dough tightly in plastic wrap and reserve it in the refrigerator for future

use for up to 5 days. Fold the circle in half, place it in a 9-inch pie plate so that the edges of the circle drop over the rim, and unfold the dough to completely cover the pie plate. Using your thumb and index finger, crimp the edges of the pie shell. Brush the edges of the pie shell with heavy cream to create a perfect, golden brown finish. Set the pie shell to the side while you make the filling.

To prepare the filling, using an electric mixer on medium speed, mix together the eggs, sugar, corn syrup, vanilla, and bourbon. Be sure to scrape the sides and bottom of the bowl at least 2 times while mixing. Add the warm melted butter and mix well. In a separate bowl, combine the pecans and chocolate chips. Sprinkle the pecan–chocolate chip mixture across the bottom of the pie shell. Pour the filling over the nuts and chips, covering them completely.

To bake, place the pie plate on a baking sheet and bake for 40 to 45 minutes, or until the pie is firm. The edges of the filling will rise, but the middle will remain a little loose. Don't worry about this—the pie will continue to bake after it's removed from the oven. Transfer the pie plate to a wire cooling rack and allow the pie to cool and set for 2 to 3 hours before serving.

If you choose, drizzle each slice with bourbon sauce to serve. Chocolate-Pecan-Bourbon Pie is best enjoyed either at room temperature or warmed at 350°F for about 10 minutes. It can be stored in the refrigerator for up to 5 days. When wrapped tightly with plastic wrap, it can also be frozen for up to 2 weeks.

Caramel-Chocolate-Pecan Pie

I don't know about you, but I take caramel very seriously. Over time, I've perfected a recipe that results in a thick, sweet caramel sauce, which perfectly offsets the pecans and flaky crust of this pie. The caramel also intermingles delightfully with melted chocolate and buttery pecans, making for a rich, dense, decadent pie. Serve with a dollop of Whipped Cream (page 193) or a scoop of dulce de leche ice cream.

level: moderate   Makes one 9-inch pie, 6 to 8 slices

Crust
1 recipe Traditional Pastry Piecrust dough for a 9-inch single-crust pie (page 5)

¼ cup heavy cream (to glaze the crimped pie edges)

Filling
1 cup sugar

1 cup dark corn syrup

4 large eggs, lightly beaten

2 tablespoons salted butter, melted

1 teaspoon pure vanilla extract

1¼ cups Caramel Sauce (page 189)

2¾ cups pecan halves

¼ cup mini semisweet chocolate chips

Preheat the oven to 350°F.

To prepare the pie shell, on a clean, lightly floured work surface, roll out half a ball of dough with a rolling pin until it forms a 10-inch circle. Wrap the remaining half of the dough tightly in plastic wrap and reserve it in the refrigerator for future use for up to 5 days. Fold the circle in half, place it in a 9-inch pie plate so that the edges of the circle drop over the rim, and unfold the dough to completely cover the pie plate. Using your thumb and index finger, crimp the edges of the pie shell. Brush the edges of the pie shell with heavy cream to create a perfect, golden brown finish. Set the pie shell to the side while you make the filling.

To prepare the filling, using an electric mixer, on medium speed, beat the sugar, corn syrup, eggs, butter, and vanilla together for about 3 minutes, or until a light brown color is achieved. Add ½ cup of the caramel sauce (if the caramel sauce has been stored in the refrigerator, warm it up in the microwave for about a minute, or until it softens and is easier to incorporate) and mix again. Add the pecans, again mixing well.

Pour the remaining ¾ cup caramel sauce across the bottom of the pie shell, spreading it out evenly. Sprinkle the chocolate chips over the caramel. Pour the pecan mixture on top of the caramel sauce.

To bake, place the pie plate on a baking sheet and bake for 55 to 60 minutes, or until the pie is firm in the middle, with just a little bit of jiggle. Transfer the pie plate to a wire cooling rack and allow the pie to cool and set for 1 hour before serving. Caramel-Chocolate-Pecan Pie is best served at room temperature. It can be stored at room temperature for up to 2 days. When covered tightly with plastic wrap, it can also be frozen for up to 2 weeks.

Light Corn Syrup versus Dark Corn Syrup

Light and dark corn syrup differ both in color and taste. Light corn syrup is clear in color, and offers a moderately sweet combination of corn syrup and high-fructose corn syrup, flavored with vanilla. Medium-brown in color, dark corn syrup has a richer, molasses flavor, based on its combination of refiners' syrup and caramel flavoring. Throughout this book, the appropriate variety of corn syrup is indicated in the ingredient list.

Chocolate Walnut Pie

Everybody loves chocolate chip cookies, so why not pay tribute to them with a pie? Biting into Chocolate Walnut Pie is just like savoring a warm, fresh-out-of-the-oven chocolate chip cookie, only even better, with a flaky crust and walnuts for an added crunch. This pie is delicious served warm with a scoop of vanilla ice cream or a cold glass of milk.

▶ level: easy   Makes one 9-inch pie, 6 to 8 slices

Crust
1   recipe Traditional Pastry Piecrust dough for a 9-inch single-crust pie (page 5)
¼   cup heavy cream (to glaze the crimped pie edges)

Filling
2   large eggs
½   cup unbleached all-purpose flour
½   cup granulated sugar
½   cup firmly packed light brown sugar
½   pound (2 sticks) salted butter, melted and cooled
1¼ cups semisweet chocolate chips
1   cup coarsely chopped walnuts

Preheat the oven to 350°F.

To prepare the pie shell, on a clean, lightly floured work surface, roll out half a ball of dough with a rolling pin until it forms a 10-inch circle. Wrap the remaining half of the dough tightly in plastic wrap and reserve it in the refrigerator for future use for up to 5 days. Fold the circle in half, place it in a 9-inch pie plate so that the edges of the circle drop over the rim, and unfold the dough to completely cover the pie plate. Using your thumb and index finger, crimp the edges of the pie shell.

Brush the edges of the pie shell with heavy cream to create a perfect, golden brown finish. Set the pie shell to the side while you make the filling.

To prepare the filling, using an electric mixer on medium speed, beat the eggs until they are foamy. Add the flour, granulated sugar, and brown sugar, beating them together until a very pale yellow color has been achieved. Pour in the butter and mix until a light shade of brown is achieved. Add the chocolate chips and walnuts and mix them in at low speed. Place the chocolate-walnut mixture in the pie shell, distributing it evenly.

To bake, place the pie plate on a baking sheet and bake for approximately 45 minutes, or until the top of the pie turns golden brown. Transfer the pie plate to a wire cooling rack and allow the pie to cool and set for 1 hour before serving.

Chocolate Walnut Pie is best served either at room temperature or warmed at 350°F for about 10 minutes. It can be stored at room temperature for up to 3 days.

Maple Walnut Pie

Because Michele's Pies was born in Vermont, I make a concerted effort to use as many Vermont products in our pies as possible—and, really, no one does maple like Vermont. The Grade B maple syrup used throughout this book is a rather dark syrup with a rich, robust caramel flavor that complements baked goods of all varieties. This pie is absolutely amazing when served with ice cream (perhaps maple ice cream) or Maple Whipped Cream (page 194).

▶ level: easy　Makes one 9-inch pie, 6 to 8 slices

Crust

1 recipe Traditional Pastry Piecrust dough for a 9-inch single-crust pie (page 5)

¼ cup heavy cream (to glaze the crimped pie edges)

Filling

1½ cups Grade B Vermont maple syrup

3 large eggs, lightly beaten

¼ cup firmly packed dark brown sugar

2 tablespoons unsalted butter, melted

1½ teaspoons pure vanilla extract

2 cups walnuts, coarsely chopped

Preheat the oven to 375°F.

To prepare the pie shell, on a clean, lightly floured work surface, roll out half a ball of dough with a rolling pin until it forms a 10-inch circle. Wrap the remaining half of the dough tightly in plastic wrap and reserve it in the refrigerator for future use for up to 5 days. Fold the circle in half, place it in a 9-inch pie plate so that the edges of the circle drop over the rim, and unfold the dough to completely cover the pie plate. Using your thumb and index finger, crimp the edges of the pie shell.

Brush the edges of the pie shell with heavy cream to create a perfect, golden brown finish. Set the pie shell to the side while you make the filling.

To prepare the filling, in a large bowl, using an electric mixer on medium speed, mix together the maple syrup, eggs, brown sugar, melted butter, and vanilla. Fold in the walnuts to the mixture. Place the filling in the pie shell, distributing it evenly.

To bake, place the pie plate on a baking sheet and bake for 40 to 45 minutes, or until the middle of the pie is slightly raised and firm to the touch. Transfer the pie plate to a wire cooling rack and allow the pie to cool and set for 1 hour before serving.

Maple Walnut Pie is best served warm or at room temperature. It can be stored in the refrigerator for up to 5 days.

Raisin Crunch Pie

At Michele's Pies we have pies for peach fans, apple junkies, pineapple aficionados, and lemon lovers. But what about raisins? Just to be sure we had something for everyone, this pie combines raisins, sweet butterscotch, and crunchy oats and pecans to create an almost candylike dessert that will hit your sweet tooth just right. This pie is delicious served warm with a scoop of vanilla ice cream and a drizzle of Caramel Sauce.

▶ level: easy   Makes one 9-inch pie, 6 to 8 slices

Crust

1 recipe Traditional Pastry Piecrust dough for a 9-inch single-crust pie (page 5)

¼ cup heavy cream (to glaze the crimped pie edges)

Filling

8 tablespoons (1 stick) salted butter, melted

½ cup light corn syrup

3 large eggs, lightly beaten

½ cup firmly packed light brown sugar

½ teaspoon pure vanilla extract

¾ cup pecans, chopped

1½ cup dark raisins

½ cup oatmeal (I use Old Fashioned Quaker Oats)

½ cup butterscotch chips

Garnish

¼ cup Caramel Sauce (page 189)

To prepare the pie shell, on a clean, lightly floured work surface, roll out half a ball of dough with a rolling pin until it forms a 10-inch circle. Wrap the remaining half of the dough tightly in plastic wrap and reserve it in the refrigerator for future use for up to 5 days. Fold the circle in half, place it in a 9-inch pie plate so that the edges of the circle drop over the rim, and unfold the dough to completely cover the pie plate. Using your thumb and index finger, crimp the edges of the pie shell. Brush the edges of the pie shell with heavy cream to create a perfect, golden brown finish. Set the pie shell to the side while you make the filling.

To prepare the filling, using an electric mixer on medium speed, mix together the melted butter, corn syrup, eggs, brown sugar, and vanilla. Reduce the speed to low and add the chopped pecans, raisins, oatmeal, and butterscotch chips to the mixture, thoroughly incorporating them. Place the raisin mixture into the pie shell, distributing it evenly.

To bake, place the pie plate on a baking sheet and bake for 45 to 50 minutes, or until the pie is firm in the middle. Transfer the pie plate to a wire cooling rack and allow the pie to cool and set for 1 hour before drizzling with caramel sauce and serving.

Raisin Crunch Pie is best served at room temperature. It can be stored in the refrigerator for up to 5 days.

Maple Oatmeal Raisin Pie

The more subtle flavors of raisin and oatmeal allow the maple to shine through, and a tinge of coconut adds a final unexpected note to this cozy combination. This pie is so simple to make, and it's a great dessert for a chilly fall night. I recommend serving this with a scoop of cinnamon ice cream or a dollop of Maple Whipped Cream (page 194).

▶ level: easy   Makes one 9-inch pie, 6 to 8 slices

Crust

1 recipe Traditional Pastry Piecrust dough for a 9-inch single-crust pie (page 5)
¼ cup heavy cream (to glaze the crimped pie edges)

Filling

3 large eggs, slightly beaten
¾ cup Grade B Vermont maple syrup
½ cup granulated sugar
½ cup firmly packed light brown sugar
½ cup whole milk
8 tablespoons (1 stick) salted butter, melted
1 teaspoon pure vanilla extract
1 cup sweetened shredded coconut
¾ cup oatmeal (I use Old Fashioned Quaker Oats)
½ cup coarsely chopped walnuts
1 cup dark raisins

Preheat the oven to 375°F.

To prepare the pie shell, on a clean, lightly floured work surface, roll out half a ball of dough with a rolling pin until it forms a 10-inch circle. Wrap the remaining half of the dough tightly in plastic wrap and reserve it in the refrigerator for future

use for up to 5 days. Fold the circle in half, place it in a 9-inch pie plate so that the edges of the circle drop over the rim, and unfold the dough to completely cover the pie plate. Using your thumb and index finger, crimp the edges of the pie shell. Brush the edges of the pie shell with heavy cream to create a perfect, golden brown finish. Set the pie shell to the side while you make the filling.

To prepare the filling, using an electric mixer on medium speed, combine the eggs, maple syrup, granulated sugar, brown sugar, milk, butter, and vanilla. Stir in the coconut, oatmeal, walnuts, and raisins. Place the oatmeal raisin filling in the pie shell, distributing it evenly.

To bake, place the pie plate on a baking sheet and bake for 40 to 45 minutes. You can test the pie by inserting a knife into the center; when the knife comes out clean, the pie is done. Transfer the pie plate to a wire cooling rack and allow the pie to cool and set for 1 hour before serving.

Maple Oatmeal Raisin Pie is best served at room temperature. It can be stored in the refrigerator for up to 5 days.

4

cream pies

Cream pies are a baker's dream because they offer a prime opportunity to experiment with a wide range of flavors: banana, cherry, chocolate, graham cracker, and even Heath bar. This chapter is a smorgasbord of over-the-top flavor.

Some of the most satisfying fruit-flavored pies actually come in cream form—Key Lime Pie (page 120), Strawberry Glacé Pie (page 124), and Twisted Citrus Blackberry Pie (page 127), for example. Not only that, but cream pies allow you to transfer other tasty flavors reminiscent of childhood such as peanut butter cups (Chocolate–Peanut Butter Dream Pie, page 104) and Heath bars (Coffee–Heath Bar Crunch Pie, page 118), into pie form.

But do not make the mistake of thinking that "creamy" is synonymous with "heavy." Pies such as Lemon Chiffon (page 122) and Coconut Cream (page 116) are light and airy treats that will simultaneously satisfy your dessert cravings and leave room for a second (or third!) slice. Finally, in this chapter, you'll put to use a range of piecrusts, including Oreo Cookie Crust (page 11) and Graham Cracker Crust (page 10), both of which lend themselves to lovely, textured pies that meld a smooth, creamy filling with a crunchy, sweet exterior.

Boston Cream Pie

Although its name says "pie," Boston cream pie is actually more of a cake, with its two layers of yellow sponge cake filled with a thick vanilla custard and topped off with a chocolate ganache. Still, it's one of the most requested items at Michele's Pies. Be sure to plan ahead a bit when making this pie because the sponge cake and cream will need to cool completely before pie assembly can begin (the cooling process will take at least 2 hours).

▶ level: moderate   Makes one 9-inch pie, 6 to 8 slices

Sponge Cake
- 1 cup unbleached all-purpose flour, sifted
- ⅔ cup sugar
- 1½ teaspoons baking powder
- ¼ teaspoon salt
- ½ cup whole milk
- ¼ cup vegetable oil
- 2 teaspoons pure vanilla extract
- 2 large eggs, separated
- ¼ teaspoon cream of tartar

Vanilla Cream Filling
- ½ cup sugar
- ¼ teaspoon salt
- ⅓ cup unbleached all-purpose flour
- 1⅓ cups whole milk
- ¾ cup water
- 3 large egg yolks, beaten
- ¼ cup pure vanilla extract

Ganache

1½ cups semisweet chocolate chips

1 cup heavy cream

Garnish (optional)

1 cup mini chocolate chips

Dollop of Whipped Cream (page 193)

1 Maraschino cherry

Preheat the oven to 350°F.

To prepare the sponge cake, in a medium bowl, combine the flour, sugar, baking powder, and salt. Using an electric mixer on low speed, add the milk, vegetable oil, vanilla, and egg yolks and beat for about 1 minute. Increase the speed to high and continue mixing for approximately 2 minutes, until the batter is smooth, with no lumps. In a separate mixing bowl, beat the egg whites and cream of tartar on high speed until stiff peaks form. Pour the egg whites into the batter and fold them together until they are fully incorporated.

To bake, pour the batter into a 9-inch greased pie plate. Bake it for approximately 25 minutes, or until you can insert a knife and it comes out clean. Transfer the pie plate to a wire cooling rack and allow it to cool completely. As the cake is cooling, prepare the vanilla cream filling.

To prepare the vanilla cream filling, in a medium saucepan, whisk together the sugar, salt, and flour. Mix in the milk and water. Place the saucepan over medium heat, and cook until the mixture begins to simmer and the cream thickens to the point where you can insert a spoon into the mixture and the cream sticks to the spoon when removed (with none of the actual spoon visible). Place the egg yolks in a small bowl and stir in ¼ cup of the heated mixture. Pour the egg yolk mixture back into the cream, and simmer for 3 to 4 minutes, stirring constantly. Remove the saucepan from the heat, add the vanilla, and whisk until it is evenly combined throughout the cream.

Pour the cream into a large bowl to cool for at least 2 hours. Note that the vanilla cream filling can be made up to 24 hours in advance. Once the cream and cake are cooled, you can begin assembling the pie.

To assemble the pie, pop the sponge cake out of the pie plate and carefully cut it in half horizontally, so that you now essentially have two layers of cake. Place the bottom layer of the cake back into the pie plate. Pour the vanilla cream filling over the bottom cake, and then place the top layer of sponge cake over the cream filling. Allow it to set for at least 1 hour before adding the ganache.

To prepare the ganache, place the chocolate chips in a medium glass bowl and set aside. Boil the heavy cream in a small saucepan over high heat. Pour the heavy cream over the chocolate chips and mix vigorously, until the chocolate chips are melted into the cream.

Pour the ganache over the sponge cake, making sure that it covers the pie completely. For extra crunch, you may also want to add mini chocolate chips along the edges of the pie. For best results, place the pie in the refrigerator and allow it to set for at least 2 hours. To serve, garnish the pie with a dollop of whipped cream and a cherry on top, if desired.

Boston Cream Pie should be served cold. It can be stored in the refrigerator for up to 3 days.

Chocolate Cream Pie

Simple and unfussy, this smooth, silky pie is pure chocolate through and through. I have several chocoholic customers who absolutely swear by it. Try the Graham Cracker Crust (page 10) as an alternative to the traditional crust.

▶ level: easy   Makes one 9-inch pie, 6 to 8 slices

Crust
1 prebaked 9-inch Traditional Pastry Piecrust shell (page 6)

Filling
¾ cup sugar

3½ tablespoons cornstarch

⅛ teaspoon salt

2½ cups whole milk

4 large egg yolks

2 tablespoons unsalted butter

2 teaspoons pure vanilla extract

3 ounces chopped unsweetened chocolate

Garnish
2 cups Whipped Cream (page 193)

½ cup mini semisweet chocolate chips

To prepare the filling, in a medium saucepan, whisk together the sugar, cornstarch, and salt. Whisk in the milk and egg yolks until they are well combined. Place the mixture over medium heat, constantly whisking and scraping the sides of the pan. When the cream begins to bubble and thicken, add the butter 1 tablespoon at a time. When all of the butter is mixed in, add the vanilla. Finally, add the chocolate a little at a time, giving each addition of chocolate the chance to melt into the filling before adding more. Keep the mixture over the heat until the chocolate is smoothly melted and the cream thickens.

Pour the chocolate filling into the pie shell. Cover the pie with plastic wrap and place in the refrigerator to cool for at least 1 hour before serving. When ready to serve, remove the pie from the refrigerator and remove the plastic wrap. Using a pastry bag to pipe the whipped cream, distribute the whipped cream decoratively across the top of the pie. If you choose, use an offset spatula to spread the whipped cream to create a more finished look. Sprinkle mini chocolate chips over the whipped cream.

Chocolate Cream Pie should be served cold. It can be stored in the refrigerator for up to 3 days.

Chocolate–Peanut Butter Dream Pie

As a fan of Reese's Peanut Butter Cups, I grew obsessed with the idea of re-creating that rich, satisfying taste in a pie and worked to develop the perfect recipe. Be forewarned that this pie is quite rich and filling. I recommend serving it at the end of a light meal—or even better, as a meal unto itself!

▶ level: easy   Makes one 9-inch pie, 6 to 8 slices

Crust

  1 prebaked 9-inch Traditional Pastry Piecrust shell (page 6)

Chocolate Filling

  ¾ cup sugar

  3½ tablespoons cornstarch

  ⅛ teaspoon salt

  2½ cups whole milk

  4 large egg yolks

  2 tablespoons unsalted butter

  2 teaspoons pure vanilla extract

  3 ounces chopped unsweetened chocolate

Peanut Butter Cream

  ¾ cup heavy cream

  2 tablespoons confectioners' sugar

  ⅓ cup creamy peanut butter

Candy Filling

  4 Reese's Peanut Butter Cups, chopped

Garnish

   2 **cups Whipped Cream (page 193)**
   ½ **cup chocolate shavings**
   1 **large Reese's Peanut Butter Cup or 8 Reese's Peanut Butter Cups Miniatures**

To prepare the chocolate filling, in a medium saucepan, whisk together the sugar, cornstarch, and salt. Whisk in the milk and egg yolks until they are well combined. Place the mixture over medium heat, constantly whisking and scraping the sides of the pan. When the cream begins to bubble and thicken, add the butter, 1 tablespoon at a time. When all of the butter is mixed in, add the vanilla. Finally, add the chocolate a little at a time, giving each addition of chocolate the chance to melt into the filling before adding more. Keep the mixture over the heat until the chocolate is smoothly melted and the cream thickens.

To prepare the peanut butter cream, using an electric mixer on high speed, mix together the heavy cream and confectioners' sugar until they create a stiff whipped cream. Fold in the peanut butter and mix until well combined.

To assemble the pie, thoroughly cover the bottom of the pie shell with chopped peanut butter cups. Spread the peanut butter cream over the candy, and then pour the chocolate cream over the peanut butter cream. Cover the pie with plastic wrap and place in the refrigerator to cool for at least 1 hour before serving.

When ready to serve, remove the pie from the refrigerator and remove the plastic wrap. Evenly distribute the whipped cream across the top of the pie. If you choose, use a pastry bag to pipe the whipped cream or an offset spatula to spread it to create a more finished look. Sprinkle the chocolate shavings over the whipped cream and either place the large peanut butter cup in the center of the pie or place 1 miniature peanut butter cup on each slice of pie.

Chocolate–Peanut Butter Dream Pie should be served cold. It can be stored in the refrigerator for up to 3 days.

Chocolate-Raspberry Delight Pie

This pie was originally called Lover's Delight Pie, and for good reason. This is the sort of dessert that you want to share with the one you love. Serve it up on Valentine's Day or at the end of any other romantic meal for two and indulge in the classic flavor combination of chocolate and raspberry.

▶ level: challenging   Makes one 9-inch pie, 6 to 8 slices

Crust

1   prebaked 9-inch Traditional Pastry Piecrust shell (page 6)

Filling

¾   cup sugar

3½ tablespoons cornstarch

⅛   teaspoon salt

2½ cups whole milk

4   large egg yolks

2   tablespoons unsalted butter

2   teaspoons pure vanilla extract

3   ounces chopped unsweetened chocolate

½   cup Fudgy Brownies chunks (page 140) or use a store-bought variety

⅛   cup semisweet chocolate chips

½   cup Raspberry Jam (page 192)

Topping

2   cups Chocolate Whipped Cream (page 193)

½   cup fresh raspberries (washed and dried)

To prepare the filling, in a medium saucepan, whisk together the sugar, cornstarch, and salt. Whisk in the milk and egg yolks until they are well combined. Place the mixture over medium heat, constantly whisking and scraping the sides of the pan. When the cream starts to bubble and thicken, add the butter, 1 tablespoon at a time. When all the butter is mixed in, add the vanilla. Finally, add the chocolate a little at a time, giving each addition of chocolate the chance to melt into the filling before adding more. When the chocolate has smoothly melted and the cream thickens, remove the saucepan from the heat and allow the filling to cool for 15 minutes. Stir in the brownie chunks and chocolate chips.

To assemble the pie, spread the raspberry jam evenly across the bottom of the pie shell. Pour the cream filling over the raspberry jam, covering it thoroughly. Cover the pie tightly with plastic wrap and refrigerate for at least 3 hours.

When ready to serve, remove the pie from the refrigerator and remove the plastic wrap. Evenly distribute the chocolate whipped cream across the top of the pie. If you choose, use a pastry bag to pipe the whipped cream or offset spatula to spread it to create a more finished look. Distribute the fresh raspberries across the whipped cream for decoration.

Chocolate-Raspberry Delight Pie should be served cold. It can be stored in the refrigerator for up to 3 days.

Banana Cream Pie

This pie is all about decadence, where the smooth and velvety filling melds beautifully with a flaky pastry crust. For optimal results, be sure to use ripe bananas as they're more flavor packed and they maximize the creamy texture that's the hallmark of a perfect Banana Cream Pie.

▶ level: easy   Makes one 9-inch pie, 6 to 8 slices

Crust

1 prebaked 9-inch Traditional Pastry Piecrust shell (page 6), cooled

Banana Cream Filling

½ cup sugar

¼ teaspoon salt

⅓ cup unbleached all-purpose flour

1⅓ cups whole milk

¾ cup water

3 large egg yolks, beaten

Filling

1 cup thinly sliced bananas

Garnish

2 cups Whipped Cream (page 193)

To prepare the banana cream filling, in a medium saucepan, whisk together the sugar, salt, and flour. Add the milk and water and heat the saucepan over medium heat, constantly whisking and scraping the sides of the pan. Monitor the mixture carefully; when it begins to simmer and becomes thick and bubbly (after approximately 4 minutes), cook for 1 more minute. Once the cream thickens to the point when you can insert a spoon into the mixture and the cream sticks to the spoon when removed (with none of the actual spoon visible), remove the pan from the heat. Place the egg yolks in a small bowl and stir in ¼ cup of the heated mixture. Pour the egg yolks mixture into the cream and simmer for 2 minutes, stirring and scraping the sides constantly to prevent burning. Remove the saucepan from the heat.

To assemble the pie, place the sliced bananas in the pie shell, making sure the bananas completely cover the bottom. Pour the warm cream over the bananas. Place the pie in the refrigerator to cool for about 1 hour. Once it is chilled, remove the pie from the refrigerator and evenly distribute the whipped cream across the top of the pie. If you choose, use a pastry bag to pipe the whipped cream or offset spatula to spread it to create a more finished look.

Banana Cream Pie should be served cold. It can be stored in the refrigerator for up to 3 days.

Mom's Banana-Coconut Delight Pie

One of my fondest memories is of making a dessert with my mom that the two of us referred to simply as "our delight." Every time I saw the pieces of this creamy banana-coconut concoction being put together in the kitchen, I would begin counting down the hours until dessert. In the years that followed my mom's passing, I made this pie only a handful of times because I could never match her recipe. Then one morning I woke up and realized I could put a twist on "our delight" by re-creating the banana-coconut cream and inserting the filling into a pecan-infused piecrust, created specifically for this pie. "Our delight" now became pure delight. Mom's Banana-Coconut Delight Pie is best when refrigerated overnight and served cold the next day. It can be stored in the refrigerator for up to 3 days.

► level: challenging   Makes one 9-inch deep-dish pie, 6 to 8 slices

Crust

- 2 cups unbleached all-purpose flour
- 1 cup coarsely chopped pecans
- ½ pound (2 sticks) salted butter, at room temperature

Vanilla Pudding Filling

- 1 cup sugar
- ½ teaspoon salt
- ⅔ cup unbleached all-purpose flour
- 2⅔ cups whole milk
- 1½ cups water
- 6 large egg yolks, beaten
- 2 tablespoons pure vanilla extract

Layered Filling

1¼ cups heavy cream

4 ounces cream cheese, softened

½ cup confectioners' sugar

1 large banana, thinly sliced

½ cup finely chopped pecans

1 cup Whipped Cream (page 193)

1 cup sweetened, shredded coconut

Garnish

2 cups Whipped Cream

Preheat the oven to 350°F.

To prepare the crust, in a medium bowl, combine the flour and the ½ cup of pecans. Add the butter and use your fingers to mix it in with the flour and pecans until you have achieved a crumbly texture. Spread the dough evenly across the bottom and up the sides of a 9-inch deep-dish pie plate. (Make sure to spread the dough uniformly so that it's the same thickness all around the pie plate.)

Bake for 20 to 25 minutes, or until the crust achieves a golden brown.

Prepare the vanilla pudding filling while the crust is baking, leaving enough time to cool before assembling the pie. To prepare the filling, in a medium saucepan, whisk together the sugar, salt, and flour. Mix in the milk and water. Place the saucepan over medium heat and cook until the mixture begins to simmer and the cream thickens to the point where you can insert a spoon into the mixture and the cream sticks to the spoon when removed (with none of the actual spoon visible). Place the egg yolks in a small bowl and stir in ¼ cup of the heated mixture. Pour the egg yolks back into the cream, and simmer for 3 to 4 minutes, stirring constantly. Remove the saucepan from the heat, add the vanilla, and whisk until it is evenly combined throughout the cream. Allow the cream to cool in the refrigerator for about 1 hour before assembling the pie.

This pie is assembled in three layers. Once the crust and vanilla pudding filling have cooled, begin assembling the first layer. In a large bowl, using an electric mixer fitted with a whisk attachment, combine the heavy cream, cream cheese, and confectioners' sugar. Mix on high speed until well combined and stiff peaks form. Spread the mixture evenly across the bottom of the cooled crust.

For the second layer, pour the cooled vanilla pudding filling over the cream cheese layer. Then arrange the banana slices across the layer of vanilla pudding. Place the pie in the refrigerator to chill for at least 1 hour before adding the final layer.

In a large mixing bowl, using a spatula, fold the remaining ½ cup of pecans into the whipped cream until they are evenly distributed. Spread the pecan-whipped cream mixture over the banana slices, covering them completely. (If you choose, use a pastry bag to pipe the whipped cream, or offset spatula to spread it, to create a more finished look.) Sprinkle the coconut over the whipped cream. Evenly distribute the whipped cream garnish across the top of the pie.

Coconut Custard Pie

Think of this pie as a coconut crème brûlée, ensconced in a flaky pastry crust. A slight hint of lemony citrus finishes it all off, adding just a tinge of unexpected zing to the rich and creamy coconut flavor.

▶ level: easy   Makes one 9-inch pie, 6 to 8 slices

Crust
- 1 recipe Traditional Pastry Piecrust dough for a 9-inch single-crust pie (page 5)
- ¼ cup heavy cream (to glaze the crimped pie edges)

Filling
- 1¼ cups sweetened shredded coconut, toasted
- 3 large eggs
- ¾ cup plus 2 tablespoons sugar
- ¼ teaspoon salt
- 2 tablespoons unbleached all-purpose flour
- 1 cup whole milk
- 1 tablespoon unsalted butter, melted
- 1 teaspoon fresh lemon juice
- 1 tablespoon grated lemon zest
- 1 teaspoon pure vanilla extract

Preheat the oven to 375°F.

To prepare the pie shell, on a clean, lightly floured work surface, roll out half a ball of dough with a rolling pin until it forms a 10-inch circle. Fold the circle in half, place it in a 9-inch pie plate so that the edges of the circle drop over the rim, and unfold the dough to completely cover the pie plate. Using your thumb and index finger, crimp the edges of the pie shell. Brush the edges of the pie shell with heavy cream to create a perfect, golden brown finish. Set the pie shell to the side while you make the filling.

Spread the shredded coconut onto a baking sheet. Toast in a 350°F oven for 2 minutes. Watch carefully as the coconut can brown easily. Toss with a spatula and toast for 1 more minute or until golden brown. Remove from oven and let cool.

To prepare the filling, using an electric mixer on medium speed, mix together the eggs, sugar, and salt. Add the flour, milk, melted butter, lemon juice, lemon zest, and vanilla and mix until thoroughly incorporated. Stir the toasted coconut into the filling. Pour the filling into the pie shell.

To bake, place the pie plate on a baking sheet and bake for 50 to 55 minutes, or until the filling is firm in the middle. Transfer the pie plate to a wire cooling rack and allow the pie to cool and set for 1 hour before serving.

Coconut Custard Pie should be served cold. It can be stored in the refrigerator for up to 3 days.

Coconut Cream Pie

Unlike a Coconut Custard Pie, which is baked and set, Coconut cream pie is a cool and luscious dessert, quite elegant in its simplicity. I've had customers tell me that its smooth taste reminds them of a piña colada. If you want a twist on Coconut Cream Pie, try using a traditional Meringue (page 39) in place of whipped cream to garnish.

▶ level: easy   Makes one 9-inch pie, 6 to 8 slices

Crust

1 prebaked 9-inch Traditional Pastry Piecrust shell (page 6)

Filling

½ cup sugar

¼ teaspoon salt

⅓ cup unbleached all-purpose flour

1⅓ cups whole milk

¾ cup water

¼ cup coconut cream (see page 117)

3 large egg yolks, beaten

½ teaspoon pure vanilla extract

½ teaspoon coconut extract

½ cup sweetened shredded coconut

Garnish

2 cups Whipped Cream (page 193)

⅓ cup sweetend shredded coconut, toasted

To prepare the filling, in a medium saucepan, whisk together the sugar, salt, and flour. Mix in the milk, water, and coconut cream. Place the saucepan over medium heat, and cook until the mixture begins to simmer and the cream thickens to the point where you can insert a spoon into the mixture and the cream sticks to the spoon when removed (with none of the actual spoon visible). Place the egg yolks in a small bowl and stir in ¼ cup of the heated mixture. Pour the egg yolks back into the cream, and simmer for 3 to 4 minutes, stirring constantly. Remove the saucepan from the heat, add the vanilla and coconut extracts, and whisk until they are evenly combined throughout the cream. Add the sweetened coconut and mix it in evenly.

To assemble the pie, pour the coconut filling into the pie shell and refrigerate for at least 1 hour, or until the pie is firm. Evenly distribute the whipped cream across the top of the pie. If you choose, use a pastry bag to pipe the whipped cream or an offset spatula to spread it to create a more finished look. Sprinkle the toasted coconut across the top of the whipped cream to serve.

Coconut Cream Pie should be served cold. It can be stored in the refrigerator for up to 3 days.

What Is Coconut Cream?

· · · · · · · · · · · · · · · ·

Chances are you'll find both coconut cream and coconut milk at your local grocer. It's important to stick with coconut cream for cream pie recipes as it has a thicker, more pastelike consistency than the more water-based coconut milk, and as a result it will enhance the flavor and texture of your filling. I recommend using the popular Coco Lopez brand of coconut cream, which is often used to make piña coladas.

Coffee-Heath Bar Crunch Pie

Coffee infuses a bit of sophistication to the rich, sweet flavor of this pie. The toffee and cookie crumb crust add a lovely crunch, which intermingles perfectly with the smooth coffee cream filling and sophisticated Kahlúa Whipped Cream topping.

▶ level: moderate   Makes one 9-inch pie, 6 to 8 slices

Crust
1 prebaked 9-inch Oreo Cookie Crust (page 11)

Filling
¼ cup unbleached all-purpose flour

⅛ teaspoon salt

⅔ cup sugar

1 cup strong brewed coffee

1 cup whole milk

1 ounce espresso (1 shot)

2 large egg yolks, beaten

2 tablespoons unsalted butter

¾ cup chopped Heath bar

Garnish
2 cups Kahlúa Whipped Cream (page 194) or 2 cups Whipped Cream (page 193) depending on preference

To prepare the filling, in a medium saucepan, combine the flour, salt, and sugar. Add the coffee, milk, and espresso, and mix well. Place the mixture over medium heat and stir constantly for 4 to 5 minutes, or until the mixture has thickened. Place the egg yolks in a small bowl and stir in 1 tablespoon of the heated coffee mixture. Pour the egg yolk mixture into the coffee mixture and simmer for 3 to 4 minutes, stirring constantly. Add the butter and continue stirring until it has thoroughly melted and incorporated into the filling. Remove the saucepan from the heat and stir in ½ cup of the chopped Heath bar.

To assemble the pie, sprinkle the remaining ¼ cup Heath bar across the bottom of the Oreo crust. Pour in the coffee cream filling, spreading it evenly across the candy. Place the pie in the refrigerator for at least 3 hours until cooled.

When ready to serve, remove the pie from the refrigerator and evenly distribute the Kahlúa whipped cream across the top of the pie. If you choose, use a pastry bag to pipe the whipped cream or offset spatula to spread it to create a more finished look.

Coffee–Heath Bar Crunch Pie should be served cold. It can be stored in the refrigerator for up to 2 days.

Key Lime Pie

This creamy, sweet, tangy pie is a southern staple. In the shop, we use only fresh key limes (they're an essential part of this masterpiece), which are imported from Mexico and Central America and are available year-round. Squeezing them does take some extra effort and determination, but it's worth all the trouble when you're rewarded with that first bite of fresh Key Lime Pie.

▶ level: moderate   Makes one 9-inch pie, 6 to 8 slices

Crust

1 partially baked 9-inch Traditional Pastry Piecrust shell (page 6)

Filling

6 large egg yolks

3 teaspoons finely grated key lime zest

Two 14-ounce cans sweetened condensed milk

1 cup fresh key lime juice

Garnish

2 cups Whipped Cream (page 193)

1 lime slice

Preheat the oven to 350°F.

To prepare the filling, using an electric mixer on high speed, beat together the egg yolks and lime zest, about 1 minute. Add the condensed milk and mix again. Reduce the speed to medium and add the lime juice. Mix for 1 more minute until thoroughly combined. Pour the filling into the pie shell.

To bake, place the pie plate on a baking sheet and bake for 15 to 20 minutes, or until the pie is firm in the middle but still soft to the touch. Transfer the pie plate to a wire cooling rack and allow the pie to cool and set for 45 minutes. Refrigerate for at least 1 more hour before serving.

When ready to serve, remove the pie from the refrigerator and evenly distribute the whipped cream across the top of the pie. If you choose, use a pastry bag to pipe the whipped cream or offset spatula to spread it to create a more finished look. Place a slice of lime on top of the whipped cream for decoration.

Key Lime Pie should be served cold. It can be stored in the refrigerator for up to 3 days.

The Key to Juicing Key Limes

. . . .

Key limes are smaller, lighter in color, and more tart than more commonly found limes. The trick to getting the most juice out of them is to pop them in the microwave for ten seconds, then roll them on the counter before juicing them.

Lemon Chiffon Pie

This pie has a lot to offer in one light and fluffy package—it's not too tart and not too sweet, which makes it a great choice for pleasing all of your guests. It is the perfect ending to a heavy meal, when you want something to satisfy that sweet tooth, but don't have a lot of room left for a big dessert.

► level: moderate   Makes one 9-inch pie, 6 to 8 slices

Crust
1 prebaked 9-inch Traditional Pastry Piecrust shell (page 6)

Filling
1 teaspoon water, at room temperature

1 teaspoon gelatin

1 large egg

2 large egg yolks

½ cup sugar

¼ cup cornstarch

Pinch of salt

1 cup fresh lemon juice

1 cup hot water

2 tablespoons unsalted butter

1 tablespoon grated lemon zest

1 cup Meringue (see page 39)

Garnish
2 cups Whipped Cream (page 193)

Grated lemon zest

To prepare the filling, in a small bowl, combine the 1 teaspoon water with the gelatin and let soften.

While the gelatin is softening, in a medium bowl, whisk together the egg, egg yolks, and sugar. While whisking, add the cornstarch and salt. Mix in the lemon juice, 1 cup hot water, the butter, and lemon zest. Transfer the filling to a medium saucepan and cook it over medium heat, scraping the sides of the pan frequently to prevent any burning. Whisk continuously until the mixture becomes bubbly and thick, about 6 minutes. Remove the saucepan from the heat and add the gelatin to the filling, folding it in with a rubber spatula until all ingredients are combined. Using a spatula, gently fold the meringue into the filling so that they are thoroughly combined. Pour the lemon filling into the pie shell and refrigerate for at least 2 hours before serving.

When ready to serve, remove the pie from the refrigerator and evenly distribute the whipped cream across the top of the pie. If you choose, use a pastry bag to pipe the whipped cream or offset spatula to spread it to create a more finished look. Sprinkle the lemon zest on top of the whipped cream.

Lemon Chiffon Pie should be served cold. It can be stored in the refrigerator for up to 3 days.

Strawberry Glacé Pie

This is a unique pie because it's not baked, thus allowing the strawberries to hold their shape and maintain their delicious fresh taste. With its combination of fresh strawberries, cream filling, and a strawberry glacé on top, this pie is perfect for a picnic or potluck gathering. Please note that the glacé part of this recipe should be made at least 4 hours (and up to 4 days) before the rest of the pie so that it has time to set.

▶ level: moderate   Makes one 9-inch pie, 6 to 8 slices

Crust

1 prebaked 9-inch Traditional Pastry Piecrust shell (page 6)

Strawberry Glacé

1 cup fresh strawberries, mashed

1 cup sugar

3 tablespoons cornstarch

½ cup water

Cream

3 ounces cream cheese, softened

1 cup heavy cream

⅓ cup confectioners' sugar

1 teaspoon pure vanilla extract

Garnish

1 cup fresh strawberries, thinly sliced, plus more to serve

To prepare the strawberry glacé, in a medium saucepan over high heat, combine the mashed strawberries, sugar, cornstarch, and water. Stir for about 10 minutes, or until the mixture thickens. Be patient, this does take time, but it is worth it. Let the glacé cool to room temperature, and then place in the refrigerator for at least 6 hours or up to 1 day prior to use.

To prepare the cream, using an electric mixer on high speed, beat the cream cheese until it is very smooth, with no clumps. Add the heavy cream, confectioners' sugar, and vanilla and mix until the cream holds its own shape and all the ingredients are thoroughly incorporated.

To assemble the pie, pour the cream into the pie shell. Cover the cream thoroughly with a thick layer of sliced strawberries. Spread the glacé evenly over the strawberries. To serve, garnish with additional sliced (or quartered) strawberries.

Strawberry Glacé Pie should be served cold. It can be stored in the refrigerator for up to 3 days.

Twisted Citrus Blackberry Pie

Although this is a cream pie, it can also be considered a fruit pie, with all the fruit that gets packed into it. Not only is the flavor combination of blackberries, lemon, and lime explosive, but its refreshing taste is perfect for warm summer nights. As an added bonus, the pie is so light you'll have plenty to go around (or go back to!). For best results, prepare the Blackberry Glacé at least 6 hours and up to a day prior to assembling the pie in order to let it completely cool and set. Also, place the condensed milk and mixing bowl used to prepare the filling in the refrigerator for 30 minutes prior to use. The assembled pie will need to be refrigerated overnight before serving, so plan accordingly.

▶ level: moderate   Makes one 9-inch pie, 6 to 8 slices

Crust
  1 prebaked 9-inch Graham Cracker Crust (page 10)

Blackberry Glacé
  1 cup blackberries, mashed
  1 cup sugar
  3 tablespoons cornstarch
  ½ cup water

Filling
  2 tablespoons warm water
  1 teaspoon gelatin
  ¾ cup fresh lemon juice
  ¾ cup fresh lime juice
  1½ tablespoons grated lemon zest
  1½ tablespoons grated lime zest
  1 cup heavy cream
     One 14-ounce can condensed milk (refrigerated for at least 30 minutes)

Garnish

2 cups Whipped Cream (page 193)

Grated lemon zest

Grated lime zest

1 pint blackberries (washed and dried)

To prepare the blackberry glacé, in a medium saucepan over high heat, combine the blackberries, sugar, cornstarch, and water, whisking continuously for about 8 minutes, or until the glacé thickens to a jamlike consistency. Place a strainer over a bowl or measuring cup and strain the glacé to eliminate any seeds. Let the glacé cool to room temperature, then place in the refrigerator for at least 6 hours or up to 1 day prior to use.

To prepare the filling, place the warm water and gelatin in a small metal bowl for at least 5 minutes and let soften. Once the gelatin has softened, place the bowl over low heat for 15 to 30 seconds and allow the gelatin to dissolve. Set the gelatin aside.

In a medium bowl, using an electric mixer on high speed, combine the lemon juice, lime juice, lemon zest, lime zest, heavy cream, and prechilled condensed milk and mix until the filling thickens, about 3 minutes. Add 2 tablespoons of the cream mixture to the gelatin, mixing them together thoroughly to temper the gelatin. Pour the tempered gelatin into the cream mixture and mix on high speed until the filling reaches a thick, creamy texture.

To assemble the pie, spread the blackberry glacé evenly across the bottom of the pie shell. Pour the pie filling over the blackberry glacé, again spreading evenly. Refrigerate the pie overnight before garnishing and serving.

When ready to serve, evenly distribute the whipped cream across the top of the pie. If you choose, use a pastry bag to pipe the whipped cream or offset spatula to spread it to create a more finished look. Sprinkle lemon zest, lime zest, and blackberries on top of the whipped cream.

Twisted Citrus Blackberry Pie can be stored in the refrigerator for up to 3 days.

5

party pies

....

The pies included in this chapter are whimsical and will likely catch your guests off guard when they are served as the pièce de résistance of a celebration. Candyland Pie (page 137), for example, offers a fun, final note to Halloween night. Eggnog Cream Pie (page 141) is a delight at Christmastime, while ice cream pies will thrill children of all ages— particularly those whose birthdays are in the warm summer months. These unique pies provide some great alternatives to more conventional celebratory treats.

Some of these pies build upon traditional foundations. Candy Apple Crumb Pie (page 135), is made much like any other apple pie, but the simple addition of caramel transforms it into a decadently gooey (and far more manageable) candy apple in a crust. Crunchy Ice Cream Pie (page 143), on the other hand, will change your guests' ideas about what a pie really is, with its cornflake-pecan crust and ice cream filling. But, boy, everyone will thank you for showing them the light.

Of course, all of the pies in this chapter are equally delicious. Whether you're making them for a full house on a special occasion or for a party of one as a weeknight indulgence, get ready to shake things up a bit with these outside-the-box party pies!

Ultimate Banana Split Pie

Every time I bite into a piece of Banana Cream Pie (page 109), I immediately start thinking about banana splits. Shortly after coming up with the cream pie recipe, it occurred to me that with the addition of just a few more ingredients, I could re-create a classic banana split, which includes bananas, strawberries, and pineapple, ensconced in a cream filling. With a Marshmallow Fluff Whipped Cream topping, a sprinkle of walnuts, and a drizzle of hot fudge sauce, Ultimate Banana Split Pie is as close as you can get to the real thing. For best results, make this pie the day you intend on serving it so that the bananas do not turn and the juices don't break down the cream.

▶ level: moderate   Makes one 9-inch pie, 6 to 8 slices

Crust
1 prebaked 9-inch Traditional Pastry Piecrust shell (page 6)

Cream filling
½ cup sugar

¼ teaspoon salt

⅓ cup unbleached all-purpose flour

1⅓ cups whole milk

¾ cup water

3 large egg yolks, beaten

2 tablespoons pure vanilla extract

Fruit Filling
1 cup Hot Fudge Sauce (page 191)

¾ cup thinly sliced bananas

8 fresh strawberries, mashed

½ cup pineapple, cut into ¼-inch cubes

2   cups Fluff Whipped Cream (page 193)

½   cup chopped walnuts

1   Maraschino cherry

To prepare the cream filling, in a medium saucepan, whisk together the sugar, salt, and flour. Add the milk and water and place the saucepan over medium heat, constantly whisking and scraping the sides of the pan. Monitor the mixture carefully; when it begins to simmer and becomes thick and bubbly (after approximately 4 minutes), cook for 1 more minute. Once the cream thickens to the point where you can insert a spoon into the mixture and the cream sticks to the spoon when removed (with none of the actual spoon visible), remove the saucepan from heat. Place the egg yolks in a small bowl, and stir in ¼ cup of the heated mixture. Pour the egg yolks back into the cream and simmer for 2 minutes, stirring and scraping the sides constantly to prevent burning. Stir in the vanilla.

To prepare the fruit filling and assemble the pie, smooth ¾ cup of the hot fudge sauce evenly across the bottom of the pie shell. Cover the hot fudge with a thick layer of bananas. Spread the strawberries on top of the bananas, and then the pineapple over the strawberries. Pour the cream filling over the fruit, covering it completely. Place the pie in the refrigerator to chill and settle for at least 2 hours.

Evenly distribute the fluff whipped cream across the top of the pie. If you choose, use a pastry bag to pipe the whipped cream or offset spatula to spread it to create a more finished look. Sprinkle the walnuts over the whipped cream and drizzle the remaining ¼ cup hot fudge sauce over the top. Place a single cherry on top of the pie and serve.

Candy Apple Crumb Pie

This pie is like one big, caramel-covered candy apple, sans the stick and a bit easier to eat. And if you are all about the crunch, add the chopped nuts to the Cinnamon Sugar Crumb Topping to really drive home the candy apple experience. This is the perfect pie to celebrate fall birthdays and other harvesttime occasions.

▶ level: moderate   Makes one 9-inch pie, 6 to 8 slices

Crust and Topping

1 recipe Traditional Pastry Piecrust dough for a 9-inch single-crust pie (see page 5)

¼ cup heavy cream (to glaze the crimped pie edges)

Cinnamon Sugar Crumb Topping (page 12)

½ cup chopped pecans or walnuts (optional)

Filling

¾ cup sugar

3 tablespoons unbleached all-purpose flour

1 tablespoon ground cinnamon

Pinch of ground nutmeg

8 medium apples, peeled, cored, and cut into ½-inch chunks

⅔ cup Caramel Sauce (page 189)

Preheat the oven to 425°F.

To prepare the pie shell, on a clean, lightly floured work surface, roll out half a ball of dough with a rolling pin until it forms a 10-inch circle. Wrap the remaining half of the dough tightly in plastic wrap and reserve it in the refrigerator for future use for up to 5 days. Fold the circle in half, place it in a 9-inch pie plate so that the edges of the circle drop over the rim, and unfold the dough to completely cover

the pie plate. Using your thumb and index finger, crimp the edges of the pie shell. Brush the edges of the pie shell with heavy cream to create a perfect, golden brown finish. Set the pie shell to the side while you make the filling.

To prepare the filling, in a small bowl, whisk together the sugar, flour, cinnamon, nutmeg, and pecans or walnuts if desired. In a large bowl, toss the apples with the sugar mixture, making sure the apples are thoroughly coated.

To assemble the pie, spread ⅓ cup of the caramel sauce across the bottom of the pie shell. Place the apples in the pie shell, distributing them evenly. Sprinkle the cinnamon sugar crumb topping over the apple filling, covering it completely.

To bake, place the pie plate on a baking sheet and bake for 15 minutes. Reduce the heat to 375°F and continue baking for 40 minutes, or until the apples are tender. Transfer the pie plate to a wire cooling rack and allow the pie to cool for 10 minutes. While the pie is still slightly warm, drizzle the remaining ⅓ cup caramel sauce over the crumb topping.

Apple pies are best served either at room temperature or warmed at 350°F for about 10 minutes. Candy Apple Crumb Pie will keep at room temperature overnight and can be stored in the refrigerator for up to 4 days.

Candyland Pie

Feel free to experiment with this recipe and include some of your favorite candy in addition to (or in lieu of) the suggestions below. Candyland Pie is a great option for Halloween, Easter, and children's birthday parties and can be adjusted accordingly. For example, if you're making this pie for Halloween, use seasonal M&Ms and add ½ cup candy corn to the topping. For Christmas, offer green and red M&Ms and mini candy canes or peppermint for garnishing. If you're short on time, substitute Fudgy Brownies with a store-bought variety.

▶ level: moderate   Makes one 9-inch pie, 6 to 8 slices

Crust
1   prebaked 9-inch Oreo Cookie Crust (page 11)

Filling
¾   cup plus 2 tablespoons sugar

3½ tablespoons cornstarch

⅛   teaspoon salt

2½ cups whole milk

4   large egg yolks

2   tablespoons unsalted butter

2   teaspoons pure vanilla extract

3   ounces chopped unsweetened chocolate

½   cup chopped Reese's Peanut Butter Cups

½   cup mini marshmallows

⅓   cup chopped Snickers candy bar

⅓   cup chopped Fudgy Brownies (page 140) or use a store-bought variety

Garnish

  2 cups Whipped Cream (page 193)

  ⅓ cup M&Ms, candy corn, candy canes, or any other favorite candy

To prepare the filling, in a medium saucepan, whisk together the sugar, cornstarch, and salt. Whisk in the milk and egg yolks until they are well combined. Place the saucepan over medium heat, constantly whisking and scraping the sides of the pan. When the mixture starts to bubble and thicken, whisk in the butter, 1 tablespoon at a time. When all of the butter is mixed in, add the vanilla. Add the chocolate, a little at a time, giving each addition of chocolate the chance to melt into the filling before adding more. Keep the mixture over the heat until the chocolate is smoothly melted and the cream thickens. Allow the cream filling to cool for 10 minutes, then mix the peanut butter cups and marshmallows into the cream.

To assemble the pie, layer the bottom of the pie shell with the Snickers and brownies. Pour the cream mixture evenly over the pie. Cover the pie tightly with plastic wrap and refrigerate for at least 3 hours.

When ready to serve, remove the pie from the refrigerator and remove the plastic wrap. Evenly distribute the whipped cream across the top of the pie. If you choose, use a pastry bag to pipe the whipped cream or offset spatula to spread it to create a more finished look. Sprinkle the M&Ms on top of the whipped cream for decoration.

Candyland Pie should be served cold. It can be stored in the refrigerator for up to 3 days.

Fudgy Brownies

. . . .

Makes 24

4 ounces unsweetened chocolate

12 tablespoons (1 $\frac{1}{2}$ sticks) salted butter

1 $\frac{1}{3}$ cups unbleached all-purpose flour

$\frac{1}{2}$ teaspoon salt

1 teaspoon baking powder

4 large eggs, beaten

2 cups sugar

2 teaspoons pure vanilla extract

1 cup semisweet chocolate chips

Preheat the oven to 350°F.

In a medium saucepan, melt the chocolate and butter together over low heat, stirring constantly until smooth. Remove the saucepan from the heat and set it to the side.

In a separate bowl, combine the flour, salt, and baking powder. In a mixing bowl beat the eggs and gradually add the sugar, mixing thoroughly. Gradually add the dry mixture to the egg mixture to combine. Stir the vanilla into the chocolate mixture in the saucepan and then combine the batter with the chocolate mixture, stirring them together well. Finally, add the chocolate chips, again stirring well.

Pour the mixture evenly into a greased 9 x 13-inch baking pan. Bake for 24 minutes, or until a toothpick inserted into the center of the brownies comes out clean. Allow the brownies to cool completely in the pan.

Eggnog Cream Pie

A unique eggnog flavor seeps through this rich, creamy pie filling, and hints of nutmeg and brandy add a cozy, wintery warmth for good measure.

▶ level: moderate   Makes one 9-inch pie, 6 to 8 slices

Crust
1 prebaked 9-inch Traditional Pastry Piecrust shell (page 6)

Filling
¾ cup plus 2 tablespoons sugar

3½ tablespoons cornstarch

⅛ teaspoon salt

4 large egg yolks

½ cup whole milk

2 cups eggnog

2 tablespoons unsalted butter

2 teaspoons pure vanilla extract

1 teaspoon ground nutmeg

1 teaspoon brandy

1 cup heavy cream

Garnish
1 cup Whipped Cream (page 193)

Ground nutmeg

To prepare the filling, in a medium saucepan, whisk together the sugar, cornstarch, and salt. Add the egg yolks, milk, and eggnog and whisk until blended. Place the saucepan over medium heat, constantly whisking and scraping the sides until the mixture starts to bubble and thicken (be careful not to burn the cream). Once it has thickened, add the butter, 1 tablespoon at a time. Add the vanilla, nutmeg, and brandy, mixing well. Pour the cream mixture into a bowl and place it in the refrigerator to chill for at least 1 hour.

Once the eggnog cream has cooled, remove it from the refrigerator. In a separate bowl, using an electric mixer on high speed, beat the heavy cream until it's stiff. Using a spatula, fold the whipped cream into the eggnog mixture until everything is blended smoothly. Pour the cream filling into the pie shell and place the pie shell in the refrigerator to set for at least 2 hours.

When ready to serve, remove the pie from the refrigerator and evenly distribute the whipped cream across the top of the pie. If you choose, use a pastry bag to pipe the whipped cream or offset spatula to spread it to create a more finished look. Sprinkle the nutmeg over the whipped cream for decoration.

Eggnog Cream Pie should be served cold. It can be stored in the refrigerator for up to 2 days.

Crunchy Ice Cream Pie

Long before the Crunchy Ice Cream Pie was famous at Michele's Pies, it was famous in my hometown of Westport, Connecticut. Whenever my mom would make this frozen treat, I was suddenly the most popular kid in the neighborhood! These are a hit at children's birthday parties, a Fourth of July gathering, or any other warm-weather celebration. Best of all on those hot summer days, there's no need to turn on the oven. Serve this pie with a dollop of Whipped Cream (page 193) and a drizzle of Hot Fudge Sauce (page 191).

▶ level: easy   Makes one 9-inch pie, 6 to 8 slices

8   tablespoons (1 stick) salted butter, melted
1   cup firmly packed light brown sugar
3   cups cornflakes
1   cup chopped pecans
1   cup sweetened shredded coconut
1   quart vanilla ice cream, softened

In a medium bowl, mix together the melted butter, brown sugar, cornflakes, pecans, and coconut. Once you have mixed the ingredients together thoroughly, separate the mixture into two equal amounts.

Take one half of the crunchy filling and evenly distribute it across the bottom and up the sides of a 9-inch pie plate. There should be no gaps between the crunchy filling and the pie plate. Stir the second half of the crunchy filling into the vanilla ice cream until thoroughly combined. Pour the crunchy ice cream filling into the pie plate.

Freeze the pie until you are ready to serve, but for at least 1 hour prior to serving. To serve, garnish each slice with a dollop of whipped cream and a drizzle of hot fudge sauce.

Crunchy Ice Cream Pie should be served cold. It can be stored in the freezer for up to 1 week.

Michele's Mud Pie

Why end a dinner party with a cup of coffee when you can end it with mud pie? This coffee ice cream–based pie with an infusion of espresso, highlighted with Fudgy Brownie chunks and a crunchy, sweet Oreo crust, is great at any time of the year. Be sure to eat a light meal so that you have plenty of room for this addictive ice cream dessert!

▶ level: easy   Makes one 9-inch pie, 6 to 8 slices

Crust
1 prebaked 9-inch Oreo Cookie Crust (page 11)

Filling
1 quart coffee ice cream
1 ounce (1 shot) brewed espresso
¾ cup chopped Fudgy Brownies (page 140) or use a store-bought variety

Garnish
Drizzle of Hot Fudge Sauce (page 191)
Dollop of Whipped Cream (page 193)
½ cup chopped almonds

To prepare the filling, scoop the coffee ice cream into a large bowl and allow it to soften. Once you can easily stir the ice cream (but before it melts), stir in the espresso and chopped brownies, distributing them evenly throughout the mixture. Pour the ice cream filling into the Oreo cookie crust.

Freeze the pie until you are ready to serve, but for at least 1 hour prior to serving. To serve, drizzle each slice with hot fudge, add a dollop of whipped cream, and sprinkle on the almonds.

Michele's Mud Pie can be stored in the freezer for up to 1 week.

S'mores Delight Pie

This pie combines all the gooey goodness of s'mores—chocolate, marshmallow vanilla cream, and toasted marshmallows—wrapped up in a graham cracker shell. The only part of the camping experience you'll miss is the smell of the fire (and maybe a few mosquito bites!).

▶ level: challenging   Makes one 9-inch pie, 6 to 8 slices

Crust

1 prebaked 9-inch Graham Cracker Crust (page 10)

Marshmallow Vanilla Cream

1¾ cups plus 2 tablespoons sugar

3½ tablespoons cornstarch

⅛ teaspoon salt

2½ cups whole milk

4 large egg yolks

2 tablespoons unsalted butter

2 teaspoons pure vanilla extract

2 cups mini marshmallows

S'mores Filling

1 cup Hot Fudge Sauce (page 191)

12 graham cracker squares

1 cup mini marshmallows

2 cups Fluff Whipped Cream (page 193)

To prepare the marshmallow vanilla cream, in a medium saucepan, whisk together the sugar, cornstarch, and salt until combined. Whisk in the milk and egg yolks. Place the saucepan over medium heat and cook, whisking constantly until the cream starts to bubble and thicken, about 4 minutes. When it has achieved a thick consistency, add in the butter, 1 tablespoon at a time. Whisk in the vanilla. Once all the ingredients have been mixed together, remove the saucepan from the heat and allow the filling to cool for approximately 10 minutes. Add 1 cup of the mini marshmallows and mix until they have melted in with the other ingredients. Pour the marshmallow cream into a bowl and let it cool in the refrigerator for at least 1½ hours. Fold in the remaining 1 cup mini marshmallows.

To assemble the pie, pour ½ cup hot fudge sauce over the bottom of the Graham Cracker Crust. Place 6 graham cracker squares on top of the fudge. Pour the marshmallow cream over the graham crackers. Dip the remaining 6 graham crackers in the remaining ½ cup hot fudge sauce and then arrange them over the marshmallow cream. Refrigerate the pie for at least 12 hours before continuing.

When ready to serve, preheat the broiler.

Remove the pie from the refrigerator and spread the Fluff whipped cream evenly over the chocolate-dipped graham crackers. Finally, arrange the 1 cup mini marshmallows over the entire surface of the pie. Place the pie in the broiler or use a kitchen blow torch until the marshmallows turn a golden campfire color, rotating the pie frequently for an even finish, about 2 minutes. Serve immediately or refrigerate until you are ready to serve.

S'mores Delight Pie can be stored in the refrigerator for up to 3 days.

Tiramisù Pie

For as long as I can remember, tiramisù has been my favorite non-pie dessert. This pie has all the rich elegance and sophistication of the beloved Italian treat, plus a flaky pastry piecrust to add yet another element to this layered dessert.

▶ level: moderate   Makes one 9-inch pie, 6 to 8 slices

Crust
1 prebaked 9-inch Traditional Pastry Piecrust shell (page 6)

Filling
3 cups brewed strong coffee or espresso
10 large egg yolks
10 tablespoons sugar
1 pound mascarpone cheese
Kahlúa to taste
2 cups heavy cream
24 ladyfingers

Garnish
2 cups Whipped Cream (page 193)
Cocoa powder

To prepare the filling, pour the brewed coffee into a bowl or baking dish, allowing it to cool completely.

In a large bowl, using an electric mixer with a whisk attachment on high speed, beat together the egg yolks and sugar until they are smooth, frothy, and pale in color. Add the mascarpone and mix for approximately 1 minute. Finally, add the Kahlúa to taste and mix some more, until all the ingredients are blended together smoothly.

In a separate bowl, beat the heavy cream until it's stiff. Using a spatula, fold the whipped cream into the mascarpone mixture until everything is blended.

To assemble the pie, layer the bottom of the pie shell with one-third of the cream mixture. Quickly dip each of the ladyfingers into the coffee (be careful not to over-soak the ladyfingers to the point of saturation). Arrange 12 of the ladyfingers over the cream mixture. Spread another one-third of the cream mixture over the placed ladyfingers. Dip the remaining 12 ladyfingers into the coffee and arrange them over the cream mixture. Spread the remaining one-third of the cream mixture over the final ladyfinger layer, smoothing out the top of the pie.

Refrigerate the pie for at least 6 hours before serving. Using a pastry bag, distribute the whipped cream decoratively across the top of the pie. If you choose, use an offset spatula to create a more finished look. Sprinkle the whipped cream with a dusting of cocoa powder, and perhaps a few coffee beans.

Tiramisù Pie should be served cold. It can be stored in the refrigerator for up to 3 days.

6

savory pies

....

Who says pies are only for dessert? Some of my favorites are actually the main course. In fact, in many cultures, savory pies such as Pizza Rustica (page 179) and Italian Wheat Pie (page 176) are a very traditional part of holiday main courses. And, though we often don't think of quiche in terms of pie, that's exactly what it is. Whether it's a special occasion or a Sunday brunch, few dishes rival the comfort of warm meat or vegetable fillings with melted cheese, wrapped up in a buttery, flaky crust.

Because you are dealing with heartier fillings, savory piecrusts often differ from their baked-good counterparts. With that in mind, each selection here has already been paired with its perfect crust accompaniment.

Making savory pies requires a bit more labor than the other pies found in this book, but think of these pies as the equivalent of a meal, rather than as a dessert. Although you will spend more prep time up front, you can save these filling pies as leftovers and get several meals out of each pie. Also, most savory pies keep well and can be made ahead, then frozen for several weeks until you're ready to dig in. Included in this chapter are tips for freezing as appropriate.

Chicken Pot Pie

I first started selling these pies at small farmers' markets in Vermont and quickly discovered just how many people share my appreciation for them. To this day, we still have a hard time keeping them stocked at the store. This is definitely a more labor-intensive recipe than some others (allow yourself at least 2½ hours from start to finish), but it is well worth it. If you're short on time, use an already prepared rotisserie chicken, and cook the vegetables for the pie in 2 cups of store-bought chicken stock. Best of all, this pie can be made as a single pie, or as individual pies as pictured.

▶ level: challenging   Makes one deep-dish 10-inch pie, 6 to 8 slices

Filling

One 4- to 5-pound chicken
5   medium carrots, cut into ½-inch slices (reserve ½ cup for pie, and the top and bottom tips for cooking chicken)
5   celery stalks, cut into ½-inch slices (reserve ½ cup for pie, and the top and bottom tips for cooking chicken)
Salt and freshly ground black pepper
½   cup ½-inch cubed potato
½   cup ½-inch cubed yellow onion
1   stick salted butter
1   cup unbleached all-purpose flour
½   cup chicken broth (reserved from cooking chicken)
1   cup heavy cream

Crust

1   recipe Traditional Pastry Piecrust dough for a 10-inch double-crust pie (page 5)
½   cup heavy cream (to glaze the top crust and crimped pie edges)

To prepare the filling, in a large pot with a strainer, immerse the chicken in cold water with the carrots and celery including tips, reserving ½ cup carrots and ½ cup celery for later use. Season with salt and pepper. Place the pot over medium-high heat. Once the water comes to a boil, lower the heat to medium and place a cover on the pot. Boil the chicken for 1 hour, or until the internal temperature of the chicken reaches 165°F (use a meat thermometer to check the temperature), periodically skimming off any fat or residue. Another indicator that the chicken is done is that the leg pulls apart easily. Once the chicken is cooked, remove it from the broth. Remove the celery and carrots and discard them so that only the chicken broth remains. Set the broth aside. Allow the chicken to cool, and then pull it apart into small bite-size pieces, discarding the skin and any bones and unwanted pieces. Measure out 2 cups chicken for the pie, and reserve remaining chicken for another use.

While pulling the chicken apart, bring the broth to a boil and add the ½ cup carrots and ½ cup celery, the potatoes, and the onions, allowing them to simmer for about 10 minutes, or until tender. Strain the broth into a bowl and set aside. Transfer the vegetables to a large bowl. Add the pulled chicken.

Preheat the oven to 425°F.

Melt the butter in a heavy-bottom saucepan over medium heat. Stir in the flour and whisk constantly for approximately 1 minute, or until the paste becomes a golden brown (be careful not to overcook the paste—you want it to be golden brown, not deep brown). Add ¼ cup of the chicken broth, continuing to whisk constantly. When the chicken broth has been incorporated, whisk in the remaining ¼ cup chicken broth. Add the heavy cream and continue whisking as the sauce thickens and the cream is incorporated, making sure to scrape the sides of the saucepan to prevent burning. Whisk until the cream has reached a thick consistency and is free of any clumps. Lower the heat and continue cooking for 1 to 2 minutes, stirring constantly. The mixture will be thick. Remove the cream mixture from the heat. Mix the cream mixture into the chicken and vegetables and season with salt and pepper. Set the chicken filling to the side while you prepare the pie shell.

To prepare the pie shell, divide the ball of dough in half, setting one half to the side. On a clean, lightly floured work surface, roll out the dough with a rolling pin

until it forms a 12-inch circle. Fold the circle in half, place it in a deep-dish 10-inch pie plate so that the edges of the circle drop over the rim, and unfold the dough to completely cover the pie plate. Spread the chicken filling evenly across the bottom of the pie shell.

To prepare the top crust, roll out the second half of the dough with a rolling pin until it forms a 12-inch circle. Fold the dough circle in half and place it over the filling, with the straight line of the half circle running down the middle of the pie. Unfold the circle so that the entire pie is covered. Using your thumb and index finger, crimp the edges of the pie together to seal in the filling, and then use a fork to puncture the top of the pie 5 or 6 times. Brush the top of the pie and crimped edges with heavy cream to create a perfect, golden brown finish.

To bake, place the pie plate on a baking sheet and bake for 15 minutes. Reduce the heat to 350°F and continue baking for 45 minutes, or until the middle of the pie is hot. Allow the pie to cool for 5 to 10 minutes before serving.

Cooked Chicken Pot Pie can be stored in the refrigerator for up to 3 days. An uncooked pie can be stored in the freezer for up to 3 months. Wrap the pie tightly in plastic wrap and store it in your freezer. For best results, thaw the pie in the refrigerator before baking as instructed.

Australian Beef Pie

In 2002 I went to Australia and fell in love with their traditional beef pies. In fact, to this day, I would have one for every meal if I had my way. Once I returned to the States, I was determined to come up with my own rendition of this classic dish. Although I created this recipe based on nothing more than my warm memories of this meal, I have nonetheless had many Australians flock to my store to purchase this little taste of home. A true testament.

▶ level: easy   Makes one deep-dish 10-inch pie, 6 to 8 slices

Filling
1 tablespoon vegetable oil
1 cup chopped onions
1¼ pounds ground beef
1 cup brown gravy mix (preferably McCormick brand)
¾ cup water
1½ cups shredded cheddar cheese

Crust
1 recipe Traditional Pastry Piecrust dough for a 10-inch double-crust pie (page 5)
½ cup heavy cream (to glaze the top crust and crimped pie edges)

Preheat the oven to 425°F.

To prepare the filling, heat the vegetable oil in a medium skillet over medium heat. Add the chopped onions and sauté until tender, about 8 minutes. Add the ground beef to the skillet, continuously breaking up the beef with a whisk to form small pieces. Cook until the beef has completely browned and is cooked through, approximately 10 minutes.

When the beef is browned, transfer the beef mixture to a strainer and drain the excess juices. Set the beef aside. In a small mixing bowl, combine the brown gravy mix and water, whisking them together until they are thoroughly combined, with no clumps. Transfer the beef back to the skillet. Over low heat, add the brown gravy to the beef, mixing well. Stir the shredded cheddar cheese into the skillet, distributing it evenly throughout the beef-gravy mixture. Set the beef to the side while you prepare the pie shell.

To prepare the pie shell, divide the ball of dough in half, setting one half to the side. On a clean, lightly floured work surface, roll out the dough with a rolling pin until it forms a 12-inch circle. Fold the circle in half, place it in a deep-dish 10-inch pie plate so that the edges of the circle drop over the rim, and unfold the dough to completely cover the pie plate. Spread the beef evenly across the bottom of the pie shell.

To prepare the top crust, roll out the second half of the dough with a rolling pin until it forms a 12-inch circle. Fold the dough circle in half and place it over the filling, with the straight line of the half circle running down the middle of the pie. Unfold the circle so that the entire pie is covered. Using your thumb and index finger, crimp the edges of the pie together to seal in the filling, and then use a fork to puncture the top of the pie 5 or 6 times. Brush the top of the pie and crimped edges with heavy cream to create a perfect, golden brown finish.

To bake, place the pie plate on a baking sheet and bake for 15 minutes. Reduce the heat to 375°F and continue baking for 35 to 40 minutes, or until the pie is hot in the middle (this can be determined by inserting a knife into the center of the pie). Transfer the pie plate to a wire cooling rack and allow the pie to cool for 5 to 10 minutes before serving.

Cooked Australian Beef Pie can be stored in the refrigerator for up to 3 days. An uncooked pie can be stored in the freezer for up to 2 months. Wrap the pie tightly in plastic wrap and store it in your freezer. For best results, thaw the pie in the refrigerator before baking as instructed.

Lobster Pot Pie

I discovered this pie while in Maine on summer vacation and could hardly wait to get back to my own kitchen to re-create it. It offers all of the comfort of Chicken Pot Pie (page 153), but with a rich, elegant lobster twist. It's hard to go wrong with chunks of lobster immersed in a creamy sauce and flaky pastry.

▶ level: moderate   Makes one deep-dish 10-inch pie, 6 to 8 slices

Filling
2	tablespoons olive oil
12	tablespoons (1½ sticks) salted butter
¾	cup chopped celery
¾	cup chopped onion
1	tablespoon chopped garlic
1½	cups unbleached all-purpose flour
3	cups heavy cream
1	cup clam juice
2	tablespoons tomato paste
1½	teaspoon chopped dill
⅓	cup sherry
⅓	cup brandy
¾	pound lobster meat (if purchasing whole lobsters, about three 1-pound lobsters yield ½ pound of lobster meat)

Crust
1	recipe Traditional Pastry Pie dough for a 10-inch double-crust pie (page 5)
½	cup heavy cream (to glaze the top crust and crimped pie edges)

Preheat the oven to 425°F.

To prepare the filling, in a medium skillet, heat the olive oil and 2 tablespoons of the butter over medium heat. Add the celery, onion, and garlic, and sauté until tender. Take the skillet off the heat and set aside.

In a large pot, melt the remaining 10 tablespoons butter over medium heat. Once the butter has melted, slowly add the flour, whisking constantly until it begins to brown. Alternate adding the heavy cream and clam juice, beginning and ending with the clam juice and whisking continuously until the mixture begins to thicken. Ultimately, you want a thick, creamy texture. If the mixture is still too thick and clumpy after all of the cream has been added, add more heavy cream or clam juice, 1 tablespoon at a time, until you have achieved a smooth, creamy consistency.

Reduce the heat under the pot to low and stir in the tomato paste. Next, add the reserved sautéed celery, onion, and garlic. Stir in the dill, sherry, and brandy, and cook for approximately 10 more minutes. Finally, add the lobster meat, stirring it thoroughly throughout the mixture. Set the filling to the side while you prepare the crust.

To prepare the pie shell, divide the ball of dough in half, setting one half to the side. On a clean, lightly floured work surface, roll out the dough with a rolling pin until it forms a 12-inch circle. Fold the circle in half, place it in a deep-dish 10-inch pie plate so that the edges of the circle drop over the rim, and unfold the dough to completely cover the pie plate. Spread the lobster cream filling evenly across the bottom of the pie shell.

To prepare the top crust, roll out the second half of the dough with a rolling pin until it forms a 12-inch circle. Fold the dough circle in half and place it over the filling, with the straight line of the half circle running down the middle of the pie. Unfold the circle so that the entire pie is covered. Using your thumb and index finger, crimp the edges of the pie together to seal in the filling, and then use a fork to puncture the top of the pie 5 or 6 times. If you're feeling creative, find a lobster cookie cutter and cut a lobster-shaped hole out of the pie top. Brush the top of the pie and crimped edges with heavy cream to create a perfect, golden brown finish.

To bake, place the pie plate on a baking sheet and bake for 15 minutes. Reduce the heat to 375°F and continue baking for an additional 40 to 45 minutes, or until the crust turns a golden brown. Transfer the pie plate to a wire cooling rack and allow the pie to cool and set for at least 20 minutes before serving.

Cooked Lobster Pot Pie can be stored in the refrigerator for up to 3 days. An uncooked pie can be stored in the freezer for up to 2 months. Wrap the pie tightly in plastic wrap and store it in your freezer. For best results, thaw the pie in the refrigerator before baking as instructed.

Quiche Lorraine

This is the quintessential quiche dish and certainly one of the most popular in the store. French farmers in the Alsace-Lorraine region of France used to enjoy this quiche as a lunchtime meal, and it's clear why. The smoky bacon floating amid a creamy cheese-infused filling is enough to keep you going all day long.

▶ level: easy   Makes one 9-inch pie, 6 to 8 slices

Crust

1   recipe Traditional Pastry Piecrust dough for a 9-inch single-crust pie (page 5)
¼   cup heavy cream (to glaze the crimped pie edges)

Filling

2   tablespoons unsalted butter (or 2 tablespoons vegetable oil)
¾   cup chopped onions
1   cup shredded Swiss cheese
½   pound cooked bacon, chopped into bite-size pieces
3   large eggs
1½ cups half-and-half
¾   teaspoon salt
⅛   teaspoon freshly ground black pepper

Preheat the oven to 425°F.

To prepare the pie shell, on a clean, lightly floured work surface, roll out half a ball of dough with a rolling pin, until it forms a 10-inch circle. Wrap the remaining half of the dough tightly in plastic wrap and reserve it in the refrigerator for future use for up to 5 days. Fold the circle in half, place it in a 9-inch pie plate so that the edges of the circle drop over the rim, and unfold the dough to completely cover

the pie plate. Brush the edges of the pie shell with heavy cream to create a perfect, golden brown finish. Keep the pie shell close by, as you will add ingredients one at a time.

To prepare the filling, melt the butter in a medium skillet over medium heat. Add the onions and sauté until they achieve a golden brown color, approximately 5 minutes. Spread the sautéed onions across the bottom of the pie shell. Top this layer with the Swiss cheese. Finally, layer the bacon over the cheese. Once you have added all three layers, gently mix them together inside the pie shell.

In a medium bowl, using an electric mixer on medium speed, combine the eggs, half-and-half, salt, and pepper. Pour the egg mixture into the pie shell, covering the onions, Swiss cheese, and bacon.

To bake, place the pie plate on a baking sheet and bake for 15 minutes. Reduce the heat to 350°F and continue baking for 40 minutes, or until the quiche is firm in the middle. Transfer the pie plate to a wire cooling rack and allow the quiche to cool and set for at least 10 minutes before serving.

Cooked Quiche Lorraine can be stored in the refrigerator for up to 3 days. An uncooked quiche can be stored in the freezer for up to 2 months. To optimally keep quiche, put it in the freezer uncovered and let it freeze on a flat surface. Once the quiche has frozen, wrap it tightly in plastic wrap and return it to the freezer.

Broccoli and Cheddar Quiche

This classic combination is great for any time of the day: breakfast, brunch, lunch, dinner or even a late-night snack. If you are partial to other vegetables, such as asparagus or zucchini, feel free to tailor this recipe to your own tastes, either substituting for the broccoli or adding more veggies.

▶ level: easy   Makes one 9-inch pie, 6 to 8 slices

Crust

1	recipe Traditional Pastry Piecrust dough for a 9-inch single-crust pie (page 5)
¼	cup heavy cream (to glaze the crimped pie edges)

Filling

2	tablespoons unsalted butter (or 2 tablespoons vegetable oil)
¾	cup chopped onions
1	cup coarsely chopped broccoli florets
¾	cup shredded cheddar cheese
3	large eggs
1½	cups half-and-half
¾	teaspoon salt
⅛	teaspoon freshly ground black pepper

Preheat the oven to 425°F.

To prepare the pie shell, on a clean, lightly floured work surface, roll out half a ball of dough with a rolling pin until it forms a 10-inch circle. Wrap the remaining half of the dough tightly in plastic wrap and reserve it in the refrigerator for future use for up to 5 days. Fold the circle in half, place it in a 9-inch pie plate so that the edges of the circle drop over the rim, and unfold the dough to completely cover

the pie plate. Brush the edges of the pie shell with heavy cream to create a perfect, golden brown finish. Keep the pie shell close by, as you will add ingredients one at a time.

To prepare the filling, melt the butter in a medium skillet over medium heat. Add the onions and sauté until they achieve a golden brown color, approximately 5 minutes. Spread the sautéed onions across the bottom of the pie shell.

Steam the broccoli in a steamer until it is tender but still firm. Top the onion mixture in the pie shell with the broccoli, then sprinkle the cheddar cheese over the broccoli.

In a medium bowl, using an electric mixer on medium speed, combine the eggs, half-and-half, salt, and pepper. Pour the egg mixture into the pie shell, covering the onions, broccoli, and cheddar cheese.

To bake, place the pie plate on a baking sheet and bake for 15 minutes. Reduce the heat to 350°F and continue baking for another 40 minutes, or until the quiche is firm in the middle. Transfer the pie plate to a wire cooling rack and allow the quiche to cool and set for at least 10 minutes before serving.

Cooked Broccoli and Cheddar Quiche can be stored in the refrigerator for up to 3 days. An uncooked quiche can be stored in the freezer for up to 2 months. To optimally keep quiche, put it in the freezer uncovered and let it freeze on a flat surface. Once the quiche has frozen, wrap it tightly in plastic wrap and return it to the freezer.

Ham and Brie Quiche

I'm a sucker for ham and brie sandwiches, thus the inspiration for this dish. This quiche is particularly rich and filling, combining the smoky flavor of ham with the creamy texture of brie. For best results, when selecting your cheese, look for a ripe brie that is less firm and somewhat mottled in appearance.

▶ level: easy   Makes one 9-inch pie, 6 to 8 slices

Crust

1 recipe Traditional Pastry Piecrust dough for a 9-inch single-crust pie (page 5)

¼ cup heavy cream (to glaze the crimped pie edges)

Filling

2 tablespoons unsalted butter (or 2 tablespoons vegetable oil)

¾ cup chopped onions

2 tablespoons cooking oil

1 cup cubed smoked ham steak (½ inch)

¾ cup thinly sliced brie

3 large eggs

1½ cups half-and-half

¾ teaspoon salt

⅛ teaspoon freshly ground black pepper

Preheat the oven to 425°F.

To prepare the pie shell, on a clean, lightly floured work surface, roll out half a ball of dough with a rolling pin until it forms a 10-inch circle. Wrap the remaining half of the dough tightly in plastic wrap and reserve it in the refrigerator for future use for up to 5 days. Fold the circle in half, place it in a 9-inch pie plate so that the edges of the circle drop over the rim, and unfold the dough to completely cover

the pie plate. Brush the edges of the pie shell with heavy cream to create a perfect, golden brown finish. Keep the pie shell close by, as you will add ingredients one at a time.

To prepare the filling, melt the butter in a medium skillet over medium heat. Add the onions and sauté until they achieve a golden brown color, approximately 5 minutes. Spread the sautéed onions across the bottom of the pie shell.

Add the vegetable oil to the skillet and fry the ham until it turns a golden brown. Place the ham in the pie shell on top of the onion layer, distributing it evenly. Layer the brie slices over the ham.

In a medium bowl, using an electric mixer set on medium speed, combine the eggs, half-and-half, salt, and pepper. Pour the egg mixture into the pie shell, covering the onions, ham, and brie.

To bake, place the pie plate on a baking sheet and bake for 15 minutes. Reduce the heat to 350°F and continue baking for 40 minutes, or until the quiche is firm in the middle. Transfer the pie plate to a wire cooling rack and allow the quiche to cool and set for at least 10 minutes before serving.

Cooked Ham and Brie Quiche can be stored in the refrigerator for up to 3 days. An uncooked quiche can be stored in the freezer for up to 2 months. To optimally keep quiche, put it in the freezer uncovered and let it freeze on a flat surface. Once the quiche has frozen, wrap it tightly in plastic wrap and return it to the freezer.

Lobster Quiche

This quiche is always one of my first picks for a summer brunch or lunchtime treat. As a New Englander, I am lucky enough to be spoiled with regular access to fresh lobster. I'm also the first to admit that the process of cooking and cleaning lobster can be somewhat arduous. To save time, I recommend purchasing fresh lobster meat (as opposed to a whole lobster) from your local seafood purveyor. Your guests will never believe how simple this elegant tasting quiche is to make.

▶ level: easy   Makes one 9-inch pie, 6 to 8 slices

Crust
- 1 recipe Traditional Pastry Piecrust dough for a 9-inch single-crust pie (page 5)
- ¼ cup heavy cream (to glaze the crimped pie edges)

Filling
- ½ pound fresh lobster meat (if purchasing whole lobsters, about three 1-pound lobsters yield ½ pound of lobster meat)
- 1 cup shredded smoked gouda cheese
- ¼ cup chopped scallions
- 3 large eggs
- ½ cup half-and-half
- ¾ teaspoon salt
- ⅛ teaspoon freshly ground black pepper

Preheat the oven to 425°F.

To prepare the pie shell, on a clean, lightly floured work surface, roll out half a ball of dough with a rolling pin until it forms a 10-inch circle. Wrap the remaining half of the dough tightly in plastic wrap and reserve it in the refrigerator for future use for up to 5 days. Fold the circle in half, place it in a 9-inch pie plate so that the

edges of the circle drop over the rim, and unfold the dough to completely cover the pie plate. Brush the edges of the pie shell with heavy cream to create a perfect, golden brown finish. Keep the pie shell close by, as you will add ingredients one at a time.

To prepare the filling, sprinkle the fresh lobster meat evenly across the bottom of the pie shell. Evenly distribute the smoked gouda and scallions over the lobster meat.

In a medium bowl, using an electric mixer on medium speed, combine the eggs, half-and-half, salt, and pepper. Pour the egg mixture into the pie shell, covering the lobster, gouda, and scallions.

To bake, place the pie plate on a baking sheet and bake for 15 minutes. Reduce the heat to 350°F and continue baking for 40 minutes, or until the quiche is firm in the middle. Transfer the pie plate to a wire cooling rack and allow the quiche to cool and set for 15 minutes before serving.

Cooked Lobster Quiche can be stored in the refrigerator for up to 3 days. An uncooked quiche can be stored in the freezer for up to 2 months. To optimally keep quiche, put it in the freezer uncovered and let it freeze on a flat surface. Once the quiche has frozen, wrap it tightly in plastic wrap and return it to the freezer.

Sausage and Provolone Quiche

Provolone cheese provides the dominant flavoring in this recipe, so select the variety carefully, according to your taste preferences. If you like a sharper taste, err toward provolone piccante; if you're in the mood for mild, provolone dolce is the way to go. The inclusion of sausage makes this quiche a great breakfast selection.

▶ level: moderate   Makes one 9-inch pie, 6 to 8 slices

Crust

1 recipe Traditional Pastry Piecrust dough for a 9-inch single-crust pie (page 5)

¼ cup heavy cream (to glaze the crimped pie edges)

Filling

2 tablespoons unsalted butter (or 2 tablespoons vegetable oil)

1 cup chopped onions

¾ pound Italian sausage (about 4 links)

¾ cup thin provolone cheese slices

⅛ cup chopped fresh parsley

3 large eggs

1½ cups half-and-half

¾ teaspoon salt

⅛ teaspoon freshly ground black pepper

Preheat the oven to 400°F.

To prepare the pie shell, on a clean, lightly floured work surface, roll out half a ball of dough with a rolling pin until it forms a 10-inch circle. Wrap the remaining half of the dough tightly in plastic wrap and reserve it in the refrigerator for future use for up to 5 days. Fold the circle in half, place it in a 9-inch pie plate so that the edges of the circle drop over the rim, and unfold the dough to completely cover

the pie plate. Brush the edges of the pie shell with heavy cream to create a perfect, golden brown finish. Keep the pie shell close by, as you will add ingredients one at a time.

To prepare the filling, melt the butter in a medium skillet over high heat. Add the onions and sauté until they achieve a golden brown color, approximately 5 minutes. Spread the sautéed onions across the bottom of the pie shell.

Remove the outer skin from the sausage by lightly cutting each sausage down the middle and then peeling off the casing. Place the sausages in a baking sheet and bake for approximately 30 minutes, or until they are thoroughly cooked. When you have finished cooking the sausages, increase heat to 425°F to let the oven preheat for the pie. Let the sausages cool, and then cut them into ½-inch pieces. Evenly distribute the sausages over the onions. Cover the sausages with a layer of evenly distributed provolone slices. Sprinkle the parsley over the provolone layer.

In a medium bowl, using an electric mixer on medium speed, combine the eggs, half-and-half, salt, and pepper. Pour the egg mixture into the pie shell, covering the onions, sausages, provolone, and parsley.

To bake, place the pie plate on a baking sheet and bake for 15 minutes. Reduce the heat to 350°F, and continue baking for 40 minutes, or until the quiche is firm in the middle. Transfer the pie plate to a wire cooling rack and allow the quiche to cool and set for at least 10 minutes before serving.

Cooked Sausage and Provolone Quiche can be stored in the refrigerator for up to 3 days. An uncooked quiche can be stored in the freezer for up to 2 months. To optimally keep quiche, put it in the freezer uncovered and let it freeze on a flat surface. Once the quiche has frozen, wrap it tightly in plastic wrap and return it to the freezer.

Spinach and Asparagus Quiche

I like to make this quiche in late spring, when asparagus is at its prime. When selecting asparagus, look for straight, firm, bright green stalks with deep green or purple tips. The fresher, the better, so purchase your asparagus as close as possible to the time you plan to make the quiche.

▶ level: easy   Makes one 9-inch pie, 6 to 8 slices

Crust
1 recipe Traditional Pastry Piecrust dough for a 9-inch single-crust pie (page 5)
¼ cup heavy cream (to glaze the crimped pie edges)

Filling
½ cup ½-inch asparagus pieces
¾ cup fresh spinach leaves
2 tablespoons unsalted butter (or 2 tablespoons vegetable oil)
¾ cup chopped onions
1 cup shredded Swiss cheese
3 large eggs
1½ cups half-and-half
¾ teaspoon salt
⅛ teaspoon freshly ground black pepper

Preheat the oven to 425°F.

To prepare the pie shell, on a clean, lightly floured work surface, roll out half a ball of dough with a rolling pin until it forms a 10-inch circle. Wrap the remaining half of the dough tightly in plastic wrap and reserve it in the refrigerator for future use for up to 5 days. Fold the circle in half, place it in a 9-inch pie plate so that the edges of the circle drop over the rim, and unfold the dough to completely cover

the pie plate. Brush the edges of the pie shell with heavy cream to create a perfect, golden brown finish. Keep the pie shell close by, as you will add ingredients one at a time.

To prepare the filling, place the asparagus pieces in a medium steamer, and allow them to steam until the asparagus is tender but still slightly firm, about 5 minutes. Place the asparagus in a colander, removing all excess water. Then set the asparagus to the side.

Wash and clean the spinach well. Place it in a medium steamer with very little water, just enough to cover the bottom of the pot. Place the pot over low heat and steam the spinach gently or until the spinach is bright green and limp, approximately 5 minutes. Drain the cooked spinach in a colander to remove all excess water. Once drained, set the spinach to the side.

Melt the butter in a medium skillet over high heat. Add the onions and sauté until they achieve a golden brown color, approximately 5 minutes. Spread the onions across the bottom of the pie shell.

Evenly distribute a layer of asparagus over the onions. Add a layer of spinach over the asparagus, and top the spinach with a layer of Swiss cheese.

In a medium bowl, using an electric mixer on medium speed, combine the eggs, half-and-half, salt, and pepper. Pour the egg mixture into the pie shell, covering the onions, asparagus, spinach, and Swiss cheese.

To bake, place the pie plate on a baking sheet and bake for 15 minutes. Reduce the heat to 350°F and continue baking for 40 minutes, or until the quiche is firm in the middle. Transfer the pie plate to a wire cooling rack and allow the quiche to cool and set for at least 10 minutes before serving.

Cooked Spinach and Asparagus Quiche can be stored in the refrigerator for up to 3 days. An uncooked quiche can be stored in the freezer for up to 2 months. To optimally keep quiche, put it in the freezer uncovered and let it freeze on a flat surface. Once the quiche has frozen, wrap it tightly in plastic wrap and return it to the freezer.

Zucchini and Tomato Quiche

Every year I find myself with more zucchini and tomatoes in my garden than I can possibly use. Fortunately, I discovered the perfect place for them in this quiche. Feel free to add in some of those other extra vegetables you may have on hand as well. Just follow the instructions for the egg mixture filling, then get crazy making vegetable selections of your own.

▶ level: easy   Makes one 9-inch pie, 6 to 8 slices

Crust

- 1 recipe Traditional Pastry Piecrust dough for a 9-inch single crust pie (page 5)
- ¼ cup heavy cream (to glaze the crimped pie edges)

Filling

- 3 tablespoons unsalted butter (or 2 tablespoons vegetable oil)
- ¾ cup sliced onions
- ¾ cup thinly sliced zucchini (approximately 1 medium zucchini)
- ¼ cup thinly sliced red bell pepper (optional)
- ½ cup seeded and ½-inch cubed tomatoes
- 1 cup shredded Gruyère, provolone, or Swiss cheese (all work well, so choose your favorite!)
- 3 large eggs
- 1½ cups half-and-half
- ¾ teaspoon salt
- ⅛ teaspoon freshly ground black pepper

Preheat the oven to 425°F.

To prepare the pie shell, on a clean, lightly floured work surface, roll out half a ball of dough with a rolling pin until it forms a 10-inch circle. Wrap the remaining

half of the dough tightly in plastic wrap and reserve it in the refrigerator for future use for up to 5 days. Fold the circle in half, place it in a 9-inch pie plate so that the edges of the circle drop over the rim, and unfold the dough to completely cover the pie plate. Brush the edges of the pie shell with heavy cream to create a perfect, golden brown finish. Keep the pie shell close by, as you will add ingredients one at a time.

To prepare the filling, melt the butter in a medium skillet over high heat. Add the onions, zucchini, and bell pepper, if using, and sauté until they achieve a golden brown color, approximately 5 minutes. Spread the sautéed onions, zucchini, and bell pepper across the bottom of the pie shell.

Sprinkle the tomatoes over the vegetables. Evenly distribute the cheese of your choice over the tomatoes.

In a medium bowl, using an electric mixer set on medium speed, combine the eggs, half-and-half, salt, and pepper. Pour the egg mixture into the pie shell, covering the vegetables, tomatoes, and cheese layers.

To bake, place the pie plate on a baking sheet and bake for 15 minutes. Reduce the heat to 350°F and continue baking for 40 minutes, or until the quiche is firm in the middle. Transfer the pie plate to a wire cooling rack and allow the quiche to cool and set for at least 10 minutes before serving.

Cooked Zucchini and Tomato Quiche can be stored in the refrigerator for up to 3 days. An uncooked quiche can be stored in the freezer for up to 2 months. To optimally keep quiche, put it in the freezer uncovered and let it freeze on a flat surface. Once the quiche has frozen, wrap it tightly in plastic wrap and return it to the freezer.

Italian Wheat Pie

This pie is traditionally served for Easter brunch. While it is sweet, it is not overly cloying. The trick is planning ahead, because the wheat needs to soak overnight. Just give yourself a twenty-four-hour head start to let the grano wheat soak, and it's a breeze from there. This dense yet moist pie can be jazzed up with plump raisins, which add even more texture to this already unique pie. I recommend using a ten-inch deep-dish pie plate for this recipe to fully accommodate the filling.

▶ level: challenging   Makes one deep-dish 10-inch pie, 8 to 10 slices

½ cup grano wheat (see page 178)

Crust

3 cups unbleached all-purpose flour
1½ tablespoons sugar
3 extra-large eggs
12 tablespoons (1½ sticks) salted butter, melted and cooled

Filling

2 cups sugar
2 tablespoons pure vanilla extract
3 teaspoons ground cinnamon
10 large eggs
3 pounds ricotta
⅓ cup raisins (optional)

Place the grano in a medium saucepan and cover with water until it is thoroughly immersed. Let it soak at room temperature for 24 hours.

To prepare the pie shell, combine the flour and sugar in a medium bowl and toss them together. Add the 3 eggs, mixing them in well, but with a light touch to avoid overworking the dough. Once the dough begins to crumble into pea-size pieces, add the butter, using your fingertips to incorporate. If the dough feels dry and is difficult to work, add a little cold water, 1 teaspoon at a time, until you are able to easily form the dough into a ball. Wrap the ball of dough in plastic wrap and refrigerate for at least 10 minutes.

When the dough is chilled, remove it from the refrigerator. Sprinkle your work surface with flour and divide the dough in half, reserving one half of the dough for the lattice topping. Roll out one half with a rolling pin until it forms a 12-inch circle, approximately ¼ inch thick. Fold the circle in half, place it in a deep-dish 10-inch pie plate so that the edges of the circle drop over the rim, and unfold the dough to completely cover the pie plate. Using your thumb and index finger, crimp the edges of the pie shell.

To prepare the filling, strain the water from the saucepan. Add new water, once again thoroughly covering the wheat. Place the saucepan on the heat and boil the wheat for 30 to 40 minutes, or until the wheat is tender and cooked through. Drain the water from the pan. Add 1 cup of the sugar, the vanilla, and cinnamon, stirring them into the soaked wheat. Set aside, letting the wheat mixture cool to room temperature while you prepare the rest of the filling.

Preheat the oven to 350°F.

In a large bowl, using an electric mixer on medium speed, beat the 10 eggs until they are lightly beaten. Add the ricotta and the remaining 1 cup sugar and mix, stopping often to scrape the sides of the bowl. If you want to add raisins to this recipe, add them into the mixture now. Add the cooled wheat mixture and mix on medium again until all the ingredients are well combined.

To assemble the pie, pour the filling into the pie shell, distributing it evenly. Roll out the second half of the dough, again to about ¼-inch thickness. Using a sharp knife or a pastry wheel, cut the round into ¾-inch strips. Place the strips over the top of the pie filling, lattice style, so that the edges of the strips meet the crimped edges of the pie shell. Ultimately, you want to create a checkerboard effect, with the lattice strips placed both vertically and horizontally across the pie.

To bake, place the pie plate on a baking sheet and bake for 20 minutes. Rotate the pie 180 degrees for even browning. Bake for 25 more minutes, or until the pie is firm in the middle. Transfer the pie plate to a wire cooling rack and allow the pie to cool completely before serving.

Italian Wheat Pie should be served cold or at room temperature. It can be stored in the refrigerator for up to 3 days.

What Is Grano Wheat?

· · · · · · · · · · · · ·

Grano is whole durum wheat and is characterized by its firm but chewy consistency. Prior to the popularity of pasta, grano served as a staple in Italian cooking. Soak grano in water overnight before using so that it can soften. Look for it at Italian specialty food shops and local grocery stores.

Pizza Rustica

Traditionally served at an Easter brunch or dinner, this pie is also a great brunch option on any day of the year. There's no doubt that this pie is a full-size meal, with its combination of a creamy ricotta base and all the meat your heart desires. There are as many variations of this recipe as there are Italian families; the following is my favorite combination. Feel free to mix and match meats and cheeses according to your preferences.

▶ level: challenging   Makes one 10-inch deep-dish pie, serves 8 to 10 slices

Crust

3	cups unbleached all-purpose flour
1¼	teaspoons baking powder
1	tablespoon sugar
1½	teaspoons salt
2	tablespoons Crisco, cold
½	cup warm water
3	large eggs, lightly beaten, plus 2 large eggs (for the egg wash)

Filling

3	large eggs, lightly beaten
1	teaspoon freshly ground black pepper
3½	cups ricotta
½	cup grated Parmesan
3	ounces sopressata, cut into ⅛-inch cubes
3	ounces prosciutto, cut into ⅛-inch cubes
2	ounces capicola, cut into ⅛-inch cubes
3	links sweet Italian sausage, broiled, skinned, and chopped
8	ounces mozzarella, cut into ¼-inch slices
8	ounces basket cheese, cut into ¼-inch slices

1 tablespoon chopped fresh parsley

4 large hard-boiled eggs, cut into quarters

To prepare the dough, in a medium bowl, lightly toss together the flour, baking powder, sugar, and salt. Add the Crisco, combining all the ingredients with your fingertips until the dough separates into crumbly, pea-size pieces. Add the water and the 3 beaten eggs to the dough, again combining the ingredients with your fingertips. As you're mixing, be aware that this dough has a different texture from most—it's a little bit sticky and has a very elastic quality to it (if the dough is sticky enough that you can't easily get it off your fingers, add a very light dusting of flour). When you are able to form a ball with the dough, wrap it in plastic wrap and refrigerate it for at least 20 minutes.

Preheat the oven to 350°F.

To prepare the filling, in a large bowl, using an electric mixer on medium speed, combine the 3 beaten eggs, pepper, ricotta, and Parmesan. Once these ingredients are fully combined, slowly add the sopressata, prosciutto, capicola, sweet sausage, mozzarella, basket cheese, and parsley. Continue to mix until the ingredients are spread evenly throughout the mixture.

To prepare the pie shell, sprinkle flour over your rolling pin and work surface, and divide the chilled ball of dough in half. Roll out two circles (using one half of the dough for each circle) that are approximately 12 inches in diameter and ¼ inch thick. Remember, this crust has a lot of elasticity to it, so really press down on the rolling pin, applying a little extra pressure. Fold one dough circle in half, place it in a 10-inch pie plate so that the edges of the circle drop over the rim, and unfold the dough to completely cover the pie plate.

To assemble the pie, spread the filling across the pie shell, distributing it evenly. Top it with the quartered hard-boiled eggs. Take the remaining dough circle and fold in half. Place it over the filling, with the straight line of the half circle running down the middle of the pie. Unfold the circle so that the entire pie is covered. Using your thumb and index finger, crimp the edges of the pie together to seal in the filling.

Break the 2 remaining eggs into a small bowl, and beat them to create an egg wash. Brush the top crust of the pie with the egg wash, taking care to cover it thoroughly. Use a sharp knife to cut at least five 2-inch slits in the top crust for ventilation (ventilation is essential for pizza rustica).

To bake, place the pie plate on a baking sheet and bake for 45 minutes, or until the crust has browned and the filling has achieved a firm consistency. Transfer the pie plate to a wire cooling rack and allow the pie to cool for at least 20 minutes before serving.

Pizza Rustica can be served warm, at room temperature, or cold. It can be stored in the refrigerator for up to 3 days.

Sweet Ricotta Pie

No Italian Easter is complete without a ricotta pie. This light, citrus-tinged pie, with its creamy ricotta filling and sweet crust, sings of spring. Although this savory pie is traditionally served as a meal, it can also satisfy a sweet tooth. There are many different varieties of Sweet Ricotta Pie (*pizza dolce*) out there, but we stick to a very basic pie that will please all palates. If you're feeling adventurous, try adding candied orange peels, grated lemon zest, miniature chocolate chips, or nuts to the filling.

▶ level: moderate   Makes one 10-inch deep-dish pie, 6 to 8 slices

Crust

- 3 cups unbleached all-purpose flour
- 2 teaspoons baking powder
- 1 cup sugar
- 1 orange
- 1 lemon
- 1 teaspoon pure vanilla extract
- 2 eggs
- 8 tablespoons (1 stick) salted butter, melted and cooled

Filling

- 3 pounds ricotta
- 1¾ cups sugar
- 10 large eggs
- 3½ tablespoons pure vanilla extract

To prepare the crust, in a medium bowl, toss together the flour, baking powder, and sugar with your hands. Using a grater, grate the orange and lemon zests into the flour mixture. Reserve the fruit of the orange and lemon for the filling. Add the vanilla, eggs, and butter, kneading them into the mixture with your fingertips.

This dough should have a smooth, even consistency, so if the mixture is still crumbly, add cold water, 1 teaspoon at a time until you can easily form the dough into a ball. Wrap the dough in plastic wrap and refrigerate it for at least 10 minutes.

Preheat the oven to 350°F.

To prepare the filling, in a large bowl, using an electric mixer on medium-high speed, beat the ricotta until it has a smooth, even texture. Mix in the sugar on medium speed. Mixing on low speed, add the eggs, 1 at a time. After all of the eggs have been added, stop the mixer and scrape the sides of the bowl. Mix again on medium speed for about 20 seconds. Add the vanilla. Either squeezing firmly with your fingers or using a citrus squeezer, add the juices from the orange and lemon (if you are squeezing the juice out with your hands, be sure the pits don't get into the filling mixture). Mix the ingredients on medium speed until they are thoroughly combined.

While assembling the pie, be aware that this dough is extremely delicate (see page 185), so be sure to sprinkle your work surface and rolling pin generously with flour. To prepare the pie shell, divide the chilled ball of dough in half. Roll out one half to a circle about 12 inches in diameter, approximately ¼ inch thick. Fold the circle in half, place it in a 10-inch deep-dish pie plate so that the edges of the circle drop over the rim, and unfold the dough to completely cover the pie plate. Because this dough is so delicate, coat your fingertips with flour before crimping the crust. Using your thumb and index fingers, crimp the edges of the pie shell.

To assemble the pie, spread the filling across the bottom of the pie shell, distributing it evenly. Roll out the second half of the dough, again to about ¼-inch thickness. Using a sharp knife or a pastry wheel, cut the round into ¾-inch strips. Place the strips over the top of the pie filling, lattice style, so that the edges of the strips meet the crimped edges of the pie shell. Ultimately, you want to create a checkerboard effect, with the lattice strips placed both vertically and horizontally across the pie.

To bake, place the pie plate on a baking sheet and bake for 30 minutes. Rotate the pie 180 degrees for even browning. Bake for approximately 20 more minutes, or until the pie is firm in the middle. Transfer the pie plate to a wire cooling rack and allow the pie to cool completely before serving.

Sweet Ricotta Pie should be served cold or at room temperature. It can be stored in the refrigerator for up to 3 days.

Working with Delicate Crust

· · · · · · · · · · · · · ·

Because the dough for the sweet ricotta pie is so delicate, it may tear during the rolling process or while being placed in the pie pan. If this does happen, you can easily solve the problem by patching up any holes or tears with dough scraps moistened with a few drops of water applied to the holes, blending together with your fingertips.

7

cherry on top

Perhaps I shouldn't give away my secrets, but the truth of the matter (as you'll soon find out in this chapter) is that making a few little extras—whipped creams, sauces, and jams—is actually quite simple. Yes, they are an extra step, but most of these recipes require no more than a few basic ingredients and ten minutes of your time.

Think of the assorted flavored whipped creams and sauces in this chapter as your "bonus round." Like varied piecrusts, glazes and garnishes not only offer up a great opportunity to finesse your pies, but they're also a chance to really cater to your guests' (or, even better, your *own*) taste buds. Although some ideas for great pairings are provided here, keep in mind the sky's the limit where your imagination is concerned.

Because these recipes don't use gelatins or stabilizers, you'll want to use the whipped creams as soon as possible (they'll keep for only a couple days). If, after finishing off that last slice of pie, you find yourself with extra whipped creams and sauces, feel free to use them to garnish and drizzle over other tasty treats, such as ice cream, hot chocolate, and French toast.

Caramel Sauce

Try this with Caramel-Chocolate-Pecan Pie (page 86) and Candy Apple Crumb Pie (page 135).

▶ Makes 1½ cups sauce

⅓	cup water
1½	cups sugar
1	tablespoon salted butter
1½	cups heavy cream
1	teaspoon pure vanilla extract

In a heavy-bottom medium saucepan, combine the water and sugar over low heat. Continue heating until the sugar dissolves, 6 to 8 minutes. Once the sugar has dissolved, increase the heat and bring the mixture to a boil, letting it simmer until it turns brown (do not stir or whisk the mixture while it is boiling—you may, however, brush down the sides of the saucepan with a pastry brush that has been dipped in water). When the mixture has browned, add the butter and then gradually add the heavy cream and then the vanilla. Stir the ingredients occasionally until the caramel dissolves and the sauce is thick and smooth. Pour the caramel sauce into a covered bowl and refrigerate for at least 5 hours.

Caramel Sauce can be kept refrigerated in an airtight container for several weeks.

Left, undercooked caramel; right, overcooked caramel; center, perfectly cooked caramel.

Bourbon Sauce

Try this with Chocolate-Pecan-Bourbon Pie (page 83).

▶ Makes 2 cups sauce

½ pound (2 sticks) unsalted butter, cut into tablespoons
1 cup firmly packed dark brown sugar
½ cup heavy cream
2 tablespoons bourbon

In a heavy-bottom medium saucepan, melt the butter and brown sugar over medium heat, whisking continuously for 6 to 8 minutes, or until the butter melts and the sugar is completely dissolved and turns light brown. Slowly whisk in the cream, and then the bourbon.

Use the Bourbon Sauce immediately or let it cool to room temperature. Pour it into an airtight storage container and refrigerate. Refrigerated sauce will keep for about 1 week.

Hot Fudge Sauce

Try this with Ultimate Banana Split Pie (page 133), Crunchy Ice Cream Pie (page 143), S'mores Delight Pie (page 145), and Candyland Pie (page 137).

▶ Makes 4 cups sauce

1 cup sugar
3 cups heavy cream
¼ cup light corn syrup
4 ounces unsweetened chocolate
4 tablespoons (½ stick) salted butter
1 tablespoon pure vanilla extract

In a medium saucepan, combine the sugar, heavy cream, corn syrup, chocolate, and butter over medium-high heat and bring the mixture to a boil. Keep the pan over heat, whisking constantly for about 5 minutes, or until the sauce begins to bubble and looks as though it is separating. Remove the sauce from the heat and add the vanilla. Transfer fudge sauce to a dish or container and allow to cool a bit before placing it in the refrigerator. Chill the sauce until it thickens, for at least 5 hours.

Hot Fudge Sauce can be kept refrigerated in an airtight container for approximately 2 weeks.

Raspberry Jam

Try this with Chocolate-Raspberry Delight Pie (page 107).

▶ Makes 4 cups jam

4 cups raspberries, pureed
4 cups sugar

In a heavy-bottom medium saucepan, combine the raspberries and sugar over medium-high heat and bring the mixture to a boil. Stir frequently as the mixture boils, for about 10 minutes, or until the mixture begins to thicken. You will know the raspberry jam is done when it thickens to the point where you can insert a spoon into the mixture and the jam sticks to the spoon when removed (with none of the actual spoon visible). Transfer the jam to a bowl, cover it tightly with plastic wrap, and let it thoroughly cool before using, for at least 5 hours.

Raspberry Jam can be kept refrigerated in an airtight container for up to 2 weeks.

Whipped Cream

With just the addition of a single ingredient, this basic recipe can be transformed into pretty much any flavor imaginable. For good ol'-fashioned whipped cream, use the following recipe.

▶ Makes 4 cups whipped cream

2 cups heavy cream
¼ cup confectioners' sugar
1 teaspoon pure vanilla extract

In a medium bowl, using an electric mixer on high speed, combine the heavy cream, confectioners' sugar, and vanilla. Mix for about 1 minute, or until a creamy consistency is achieved. You'll know it's ready when you can form stiff peaks using a spatula.

For best results, whipped cream should be used on the same day it is made.

Chocolate Whipped Cream

Try this with Chocolate Cream Pie (page 102), Chocolate-Raspberry Delight Pie (page 107), and Candyland Pie (page 137).

Prior to preparation, place a metal bowl in the freezer to chill for at least 15 minutes. Once the bowl is chilled, add ¼ cup cooled Hot Fudge Sauce (page 191) to the basic whipped cream ingredients and prepare as directed.

Fluff Whipped Cream

Try this with Ultimate Banana Split Pie (page 133) and S'mores Delight Pie (page 145).

Prior to preparation, place a metal bowl in the freezer to chill for at least 15 minutes. Once the bowl is chilled, add ½ cup Marshmallow Fluff to the basic whipped cream ingredients and prepare as directed.

Kahlúa Whipped Cream

Try this with Coffee–Heath Bar Crunch Pie (page 118).

Prior to preparation, place a metal bowl in the freezer to chill for at least 15 minutes. Once the bowl is chilled, add 2 tablespoons Kahlúa (or more to taste) to the basic whipped cream ingredients and prepare as directed.

Maple Whipped Cream

Try this with Maple Pumpkin Pie with Pecan Streusel (page 62), and Maple Walnut Pie (page 90).

Prior to preparation, place a metal bowl in the freezer to chill for at least 15 minutes. Once the bowl is chilled, add ½ cup maple syrup (or more to taste) to the basic whipped cream ingredients and prepare as directed.

How to Create the Perfect Whipped Cream Consistency

Achieving the correct whipped cream consistency is the trick to a perfect cream pie. There's an easy way to determine exactly when your cream has reached this just-right consistency: Pull your whisk attachment (or a spatula) straight up out of the cream—the peak of the cream should hold its shape and stick tightly to the whisk. Once you have achieved these stiff peaks, stop beating immediately. Continuing to beat the cream after this point will cause it to separate and curdle.

Acknowledgments

Thanks to my editor, Pamela Cannon, for her detailed eye and dedication to this project, and to the phenomenal Ballantine team, including Libby McGuire, Susan Corcoran, Porscha Burke, Anna Bauer, and Diane Hobbing. To my agent, Coleen O'Shea, for discovering my shop and finding the perfect home for this book. Thanks to Ben Fink for his beautiful photographs, which make me and my pies look so good, and to Nikki Van Noy for seeing this project through from start to finish.

To my staff, for their ceaseless dedication to my business.

A huge thanks to my family and friends for all of their support and patience while I opened and grew Michele's Pies. Thanks to my loving dad, who, along with Ruth, has been behind me every step of the way, offering countless hours of help. A very heartfelt thank you to the Stuart family for their love and support—and especially for standing by my side at every National Pie Championships competition. Thanks to my stepson, Dakota, for his never-ending patience and enthusiasm.

And, of course, to my husband and Michele's Pies co-founder, Kelly Stuart, who truly understands my dedication to the pie business and who has been there for me since the beginning. Without his help and perseverance, Michele's Pies may never have been born in the first place.

Index

A

adjustable measuring cups, xvi

apples
    Apple-Cranberry Crumb Pie, 23–24
    Apple-Raspberry Pie, 20
    Candy Apple Crumb Pie, 135–36
    Country Apple Pie, 19–20
    Pear-Apple-Cranberry Crumb Pie, 51–52
    Sugar-Free Apple Pie, 21–22

Asparagus and Spinach Quiche, 171–72

Australian Beef Pie, 156–57

B

baking sheets, xviii

bananas
    Banana Cream Pie, 109–10
    Mom's Banana-Coconut Delight Pie, 111–13
    Ultimate Banana Split Pie, 133–34

basic ingredients, xix

Beef Pie, Australian, 156–57

Best Pie in America: Best Slice Challenge, xiii, 79, 83

blackberries
    Blackberry Pie, 25–26
    Blueberry-Blackberry Crumb Pie, 32–33
    Twisted Citrus Blackberry Pie, 127–28

blueberries
    Blueberry-Blackberry Crumb Pie, 32–33
    Blueberry Pie, 27–29
    Peach-Blueberry Pie, 45–46
    Sugar-Free Blueberry Pie, 30–31

Boston Cream Pie, 99–101

Bourbon Sauce, 83–84, 190

Brie and Ham Quiche, 165–66

Broccoli and Cheddar Quiche, 163–64

brushes, xvi

butter, xix, 7

C

Candy Apple Crumb Pie, 135–36

Candyland Pie, 137–39

Caramel Sauce, 87, 189
    Candy Apple Crumb Pie, 135–36
    Caramel-Chocolate Pecan Pie, 86–87
    Raisin Crunch Pie, 92–93

challenging pies, xv

Cheddar and Broccoli Quiche, 163–64

cheese
    Broccoli and Cheddar Quiche, 163–64
    Ham and Brie Quiche, 165–66
    Italian Wheat Pie, 176–78
    Lobster Quiche, 167–68
    Pizza Rustica, 179–81
    Quiche Lorraine, 161–62
    Sausage and Provolone Quiche, 169–70
    Spinach and Asparagus Quiche, 171–72
    Sweet Ricotta Pie, 183–85
    Zucchini and Tomato Quiche, 173–75

cherries
    Cherry Pie, 34–35
    Sour Cherry Crunch Pie, 37–38

Chicken Pot Pie, 153–55

chiffon pies
    Lemon Chiffon Pie, 122–23
    Pumpkin Chiffon Pie, 66–67
chocolate
    Boston Cream Pie, 99–101
    Chocolate Cream Pie, 102–3
    Chocolate-Peanut Butter Dream Pie,
      104–5
    Chocolate-Pecan-Bourbon Pie, xiii,
      79, 83–84
    Chocolate-Raspberry Delight Pie,
      107–8
    Chocolate Walnut Pie, 88–89
    Chocolate Whipped Cream, 107, 193
    Fudgy Brownies, 140
    ganache, 100–101
    Tiramisù Pie, 147–49
Cinnamon Sugar Crumb Topping, 12
    Apple-Cranberry Crumb Pie, 23–24
    Blueberry-Blackberry Crumb Pie,
      32–33
    Candy Apple Crumb Pie, 135–36
    Peach Crumb Pie, 43–44
    Pear-Apple-Cranberry Crumb Pie,
      51–52
    Pineapple Crumb Pie, 55–56
    Raspberry Crumb Pie, 69–70
    Strawberry-Rhubarb Crumb Pie,
      73–74
coconut
    Coconut Cream Pie, 116–17
    Coconut Custard Pie, 114–15
    Macadamia-Coconut Crumb Topping,
      13, 57–58
    Mom's Banana-Coconut Delight Pie,
      111–13
coffee
    Michele's Mud Pie, 144
    Tiramisù Pie, 147–49

Coffee–Heath Bar Crunch Pie, 118–19
cornflakes, 143
corn syrup, 87
Country Apple Pie, 19–20
cranberries, 52
    Apple-Cranberry Crumb Pie, 23–24
    Pear-Apple-Cranberry Crumb Pie,
      51–52
    Pear-Cranberry Pie with Walnut
      Crumb, 53–54
cream filling, vanilla, 99–100
Crisco, xix, 7
Crunchy Ice Cream Pie, 143
crusts, 3–11
    baking, 24
    crimping, 9
    flakiness, 7
    Graham Cracker Crust, 10
    lattice tops, 35–36
    Oreo Cookie Crust, 11
    overhandling, 5
    pecan crust, 111–12
    puncture patterns, 31
    repairing, 185
    Traditional Pastry Piecrust, 5–9

D

dark corn syrup, 87
deep-dish plates, xvii
dough. *See* crusts

E

easy pies, xv
Eggnog Cream Pie, 141–42
espresso
    Michele's Mud Pie, 144
    Tiramisù Pie, 147–49

F

Flay, Bobby, xiv
flour, xix
Fluff Whipped Cream, 134, 145–46, 193
food processors, xviii
freezing pie crusts, 6
Fudgy Brownies, 140
    Candyland Pie, 137–39
    Chocolate-Raspberry Delight Pie, 107
    Michele's Mud Pie, 144

G

ganache, 100–101
Graham Cracker Crust, 10
    S'mores Delight Pie, 145–46
    Twisted Citrus Blackberry Pie,
      127–28
grano wheat, 176, 178
graters, xviii

H

Ham and Brie Quiche, 165–66
hand graters, xviii
Hot Fudge Sauce, 133, 191
    Michele's Mud Pie, 144
    S'mores Delight Pie, 145–46

I

ice cream
    Crunchy Ice Cream Pie, 143
    Michele's Mud Pie, 144
Italian Wheat Pie, 176–78

J

juicers, xviii

K

Kahlúa Whipped Cream, 118, 194
Key Lime Pie, 120–21
kitchen tools, xvi–xviii
kitchen torches, xviii

L

ladyfingers, 147–49
lattice top crusts, 35–36
lemon
    Lemon Chiffon Pie, 122–23
    Lemon Meringue Pie, 39–41
light corn syrup, 87
lobster
    Lobster Pot Pie, 158–60
    Lobster Quiche, 167–68
Lorraine, Quiche, 161–62

M

Macadamia-Coconut Crumb Topping, 13,
    57–58
Madagascar vanilla, xix
Mango-Pineapple Pie with Macadamia-
    Coconut Crumb, 57–58
maple syrup
    Maple Oatmeal Raisin Pie, 94–95
    Maple Pumpkin Pie with Pecan
      Streusel, xiv, 62–64
    Maple Walnut Pie, 90–91
    Maple Whipped Cream, 194
Marshmallow Vanilla Cream, 145–46
measuring cups, xvi
meat
    Australian Beef Pie, 156–57
    Chicken Pot Pie, 153–55
    Pizza Rustica, 179–81
    Sausage and Provolone Quiche, 169–70

meringue, 39–41
Michele's Mud Pie, 144
Michele's Pies, xi, xiii–xiv, 203
microplanes, xviii
milk, xix
moderate pies, xv
Mom's Banana-Coconut Delight Pie,
    111–13

N
National Pie Championship Awards, xi,
    xiii–xiv
    Apple-Cranberry Crumb Pie, 23–24
    Blueberry-Blackberry Pie, 32–33
    Chocolate-Peanut Butter Dream Pie,
      104–5
    Chocolate-Pecan-Bourbon Pie, 83–84
    Coconut Cream Pie, 116–17
    Coconut Custard Pie, 114–15
    Country Apple Pie, 19–20
    Pecan Pie, 81–82
    Pumpkin Pie, 59–61
    Sugar-Free Apple Pie, 21–22
National Pie Day, 21

O
offset spatulas, xviii
Oreo Cookie Crust, 11
    Candyland Pie, 137–39
    Coffee-Heath Bar Crunch Pie, 118–19
    Michele's Mud Pie, 144
overhandling, 5

P
partially baked pie shells, 6–7
pastry bags, xviii

pastry blenders, xvi
pastry brushes, xvi
pastry tips, xviii–xix
peaches
    Peach-Blueberry Pie, 45–46
    Peach Crumb Pie, 43–44
    peeling, 44
Peanut Butter-Chocolate Dream Pie, 104–5
pears
    Pear-Apple-Cranberry Crumb Pie,
      51–52
    Pear-Cranberry Pie with Walnut
      Crumb, 53–54
    Pear Pie, 47–48
    Pear-Raspberry Pie, 49–50
pecans
    Caramel-Chocolate Pecan Pie, 86–87
    Chocolate-Pecan-Bourbon Pie, xiii,
      79, 83–84
    Crunchy Ice Cream Pie, 143
    crust, 111–12
    Pecan Pie, 81–82
    Pecan Streusel, 62–63
    Raisin Crunch Pie, 92–93
pie plates, xvii
pie pumpkins, 64–65
pie shells, 4
pie weights, xvii, 9
pineapples
    Pineapple Crumb Pie, 55–56
    Pineapple-Mango Pie with
      Macadamia-Coconut Crumb, 57–58
    Ultimate Banana Split Pie, 133–34
Pizza Rustica, 179–81
pot pies
    Chicken, 153–55
    Lobster, 158–60
prebaked pie shells, 6–7
Provolone and Sausage Quiche, 169–70

pumpkin
    Maple Pumpkin Pie with Pecan
        Streusel, 62–64
    Pumpkin Chiffon Pie, 66–67
    Pumpkin Pie, 59–61
    purée, 65
    sugar pumpkins, 64–65
puncture patterns, 31

Q

quiche
    Broccoli and Cheddar, 163–64
    Ham and Brie, 165–66
    Lobster, 167–68
    Lorraine, 161–62
    Sausage and Provolone, 169–70
    Spinach and Asparagus Quiche,
        171–72
    Zucchini and Tomato, 173–75

R

raisins
    Maple Oatmeal Raisin Pie, 94–95
    Raisin Crunch Pie, 92–93
raspberries
    Apple-Raspberry Pie, 20
    Chocolate-Raspberry Delight Pie,
        107–8
    Pear-Raspberry Pie, 49–50
    Raspberry Crumb Pie, 69–70
    Raspberry Jam, 107, 192
rhubarb
    Rhubarb Pie, 71–72
    Strawberry-Rhubarb Crumb Pie,
        73–74
ricotta
    Italian Wheat Pie, 176–78

Pizza Rustica, 179–81
Sweet Ricotta Pie, 183–85
rolling pins, xvii–xviii

S

sauces
    Bourbon Sauce, 83–84, 190
    Caramel Sauce, 86–87, 92–93, 135–36,
        189
    Hot Fudge Sauce, 133, 144, 145–46,
        191
    See also toppings; whipped cream
Sausage and Provolone Quiche, 169–70
scooping and sweeping, xvi
seafood
    Lobster Pot Pie, 158–60
    Lobster Quiche, 167–68
shortening, xix, 7
single-crust pies, 6
S'mores Delight Pie, 145–46
Sour Cherry Crunch Pie, 37–38
spatulas, xviii
Spinach and Asparagus Quiche,
    171–72
Splenda, 21
sponge cake, 99–100
strawberries
    Strawberry Glacé Pie, 124–25
    Strawberry-Rhubarb Crumb Pie,
        73–74
    Ultimate Banana Split Pie, 133–34
streusel, pecan, 62–63
sugar-free pies
    Apple Pie, 21–22
    Blueberry, 30–31
sugar pumpkins, 64–65
Sweet Potato Pie, 75–76
Sweet Ricotta Pie, 183–85

T

Tiramisù Pie, 147–49

Tomato and Zucchini Quiche, 173–75

toppings, 3, 4, 12–14

    Cinnamon Sugar Crumb Topping, 12

    Macadamia-Coconut Crumb Topping, 13

    meringue, 39–41

    Pecan Streusel, 62–63

    Walnut Crumb Topping, 14

    See also sauces; whipped cream

Traditional Pastry Piecrust, 5–9

Twisted Citrus Blackberry Pie, 127–28

U

Ultimate Banana Split Pie, 133–34

V

vanilla cream filling, 99–100

vanilla extract, xix

W

walnuts

    Chocolate Walnut Pie, 88–89

    Maple Oatmeal Raisin Pie, 94–95

    Maple Walnut Pie, 90–91

    Ultimate Banana Split Pie, 133–34

    Walnut Crumb Topping, 14, 37–38, 53–54

weights, xvii, 9

Wheat Pie, Italian, 176–78

whipped cream, 193–94

    Chocolate Whipped Cream, 107, 193

    Fluff Whipped Cream, 134, 145–46, 193

    Kahlúa Whipped Cream, 118

    Maple Whipped Cream, 194

    See also sauces

Z

zesters, xviii

Zucchini and Tomato Quiche, 173–75

About the Author

MICHELE STUART is the owner and pastry chef of Michele's Pies in Norwalk, Connecticut, and Westport, Connecticut. Her pies have earned her twenty-six National Pie Championships Awards in the commercial category and two first-place awards in the professional category. Michele and her pies have been featured in or on *The New York Times, Good Morning America,* and the Food Network, among other media outlets.